COMMUNICATING EFFECTIVELY ON TELEVISION

Wadsworth Series in Mass Communication
Rebecca Hayden, Senior Editor

GENERAL

The New Communications by Frederick Williams

Mediamerica: Form, Content, and Consequence of Mass Communication, 3d, by Edward Jay Whetmore

The Interplay of Influence: Mass Media & Their Publics in News, Advertising, Politics by Kathleen Hall Jamieson and Karlyn Kohrs Campbell

Mass Communication and Everyday Life: A Perspective on Theory and Effects by Dennis K. Davis and Stanley J. Baran

Mass Media Research: An Introduction by Roger D. Wimmer and Joseph R. Dominick

The Internship Experience by Lynne Schafer Gross

TELECOMMUNICATIONS

Stay Tuned: A Concise History of American Broadcasting by Christopher H. Sterling and John M. Kittross

Writing for Television and Radio, 4th, by Robert L. Hilliard

Communicating Effectively on Television by Evan Blythin and Larry A. Samovar

Broadcast/Cable Programming: Strategies and Practices, 2d, by Susan Tyler Eastman, Sydney W. Head, and Lewis Klein

Advertising in the Broadcast and Cable Media, 2d, by Elizabeth J. Heighton and Don R. Cunningham

Strategies in Broadcast and Cable Promotion by Susan Tyler Eastman and Robert A. Klein

Modern Radio Station Practices, 2d, by Joesph S. Johnson and Kenneth K. Jones

The Magic Medium: An Introduction to Radio in America by Edward Jay Whetmore

Audio in Media by Stanley R. Alten

Television Production Handbook, 4th, by Herbert Zettl

Sight-Sound-Motion: Applied Media Aesthetics by Herbert Zettl

Electronic Cinematography: Achieving Photographic Control over the Video Image by Harry Mathias and Richard Patterson

JOURNALISM

Media Writing: News for the Mass Media by Doug Newsom and James A. Wollert

Excellence in College Journalism by Wayne Overbeck and Thomas M. Pasqua

When Words Collide: A Journalist's Guide to Grammar & Style by Lauren Kessler and Duncan McDonald

News Editing in the '80s: Text and Exercises by William L. Rivers

Reporting Public Affairs: Problems and Solutions by Ronald P. Lovell

Newswriting for the Electronic Media: Principles, Examples, Applications by Daniel E. Garvey and William L. Rivers

Free-Lancer and Staff Writer: Newspaper Features and Magazine Articles, 3rd, by William L. Rivers and Shelley Smolkin

Magazine Editing in the '80s: Text and Exercises by William L. Rivers

This is PR: The Realities of Public Relations, 3rd, by Doug Newsom and Alan Scott

Writing in Public Relations Practice: Form and Style by Doug Newsom and Tom Siegfried

Creative Strategy in Advertising, 2d, by A. Jerome Jewler

COMMUNICATING EFFECTIVELY ON TELEVISION

EVAN BLYTHIN
University of Nevada, Las Vegas

LARRY A. SAMOVAR
San Diego State University

WADSWORTH PUBLISHING COMPANY
A Division of Wadsworth, Inc.
Belmont, California

Senior Editor: Rebecca Hayden
Production Editor: Leland Moss
Managing Designers: Detta Penna and Andrew H. Ogus
Designer: Kathy Flanders
Copy Editor: Anne Montague
Technical Illustrator: Salinda Tyson
Cover: Andrew H. Ogus

Printed in the United States of America

1 2 3 4 5 6 7 8 9 10—89 88 87 86 85

ISBN 0-534-03355-5

Library of Congress Cataloging in Publication Data

Blythin, Evan.
  Communicating effectively on television.

  Includes index.
  1. Interviewing in television.   I. Samovar, Larry A.
II. Title.
PN1992.8.I68B59 1985   791.45'0141   84–3648
ISBN 0–534–03355–5

Photo Credits

Figures 1.1, 1.2, 7.1, 7.2, 7.3, 9.1, 10.1, 10.3, photography by Kira Corser, courtesy KPBS, Channel 15, San Diego, California.

Figures 2.1, 7.5, 7.8, 8.8, 9.2, 11.1, photography courtesy Robert Lee, Department of Telecommunications and Film, San Diego State University.

Figures 2.2, 7.4, 7.7, 10.2, 12.1, *Over Easy* promotional photos, courtesy of Power/Rector Productions and KQED, Inc.

Figure 8.1, courtesy RCA.

Figures 8.2, 8.5, courtesy Angenieux, Inc.

Figures 8.3, 8.4, photographs by Herbert Zettl from *Television Production Handbook, Fourth Edition,* courtesy Wadsworth Publishing Company.

Figure 8.5, courtesy Electro-Voice.

Figure 8.7, courtesy AKG Acoustics, Inc., Stamford, Connecticut.

CONTENTS

PREFACE

In writing this book, our primary interest is not what television does to us, but what we do with television. We no longer live in an era when people simply sit in front of their television sets and passively watch others "perform"; we are approaching the point when active participation in television will be a mark of literacy. This book seeks to describe, explain, and contribute to that literacy—in short, to assist people to become effective communicators on television.

Focus

Most books written about television are aimed at people who are, or plan to be, technicians or actors. Our text is written for a somewhat different reader—the person who, because of career or circumstance, will be facing the eye of the camera. These people might be educators, lawyers, doctors, business persons, engineers, or politicians. Their specific occupations are not important. What is important is that they will be appearing on television as part of their professional lives.

Television is also becoming a medium of personal expression and purpose. This book will serve both the personal and professional needs of people interested in communicating effectively on television.

Approach

Communication is a shared activity, something we do with one another. Our approach is, therefore, practical rather than theoretical. We offer advice and information that we hope will enable you to communicate your message better to other people.

Organization

We have organized this book around a sequence that follows the same steps you would follow if you were going to appear on television. Part One stresses the idea that as a starting point you should know your personal objectives as well as the possible objectives of television communication. Getting started also means that you must understand your co-

communicators. In Part One we discuss how you may identify your co-communicators and adapt your message to their specific backgrounds and needs.

Parts Two and Three focus on television messages. Having something to say (content) and a clear way of saying it (organization) are parts of effective television communication. Part Four presents information that introduces you to the television studio. Part Five takes you in front of the camera; we discuss the visual and auditory dimensions of televising yourself and your message.

In Part Six we focus on a particularly common form of television presentation, and offer practical advice on successful television interviewing.

Finally, at the end of this book we ask you to consider the responsibilities that go along with television communication and your potential influence and impact as a television communicator.

Special Features

Each section of this book begins with a preview. Knowing what is coming enables you to see how all the small pieces fit together. Each section ends with a series of features designed to take you beyond this book. We recommend readings on the topics treated in each section should you wish supplemental information. And we provide a form with which you can evaluate your television presentations as well as the presentations of other people; the form also serves as a useful summary of the content of the chapters involved.

Collaborators

Throughout this book we talk about the collaborative nature of television. This book is also the product of a collaborative process:

> We are indebted to one another for the perseverance that brings this work to fruition.
> We are in debt to Becky Hayden for her diligence and her steady guidance.
> Credit is due to Steve King for helping Larry find time, and to John Unrue and Jim Adams who did the same for Evan.
> Credit is also due to Kay Grinnell and to Jack Mills for abiding editorial and technical assistance.

Special Projects Editors Autumn Stanley and Steven Robins, Copy Editor Anne Montague, and Production Editor Leland Moss have been invaluable in making this book a reality.

Finally, we owe an account to those people who reviewed the manuscript in its early stages. They saved us much grief and embarrassment; we appreciate their time and concern. Our thanks go to Cary B. Bell, California State University, Sacramento; Gil Clardy, East Texas State University; Gary Copeland, University of Alabama; Juliet L. Dee, University of California, Santa Barbara; Dennis A. Harp, Texas Tech University; and Richard Lucas, Southern Connecticut State University.

COMMUNICATING EFFECTIVELY ON TELEVISION

PART ONE

TELEVISION AND HUMAN AFFAIRS

If you are thirty years old, in business or the professions, the chances of your avoiding an appearance on television are nearly zero.

Jack Hilton
The Wall Street Journal

Our own experiences have been the driving force behind this book. After using and examining television in our personal and public lives, we have come to the conclusion that television is rapidly becoming a principal medium of communication in human affairs.

In Chapter 1 we will talk about opportunities for the personal use of television and about the people who are currently taking advantage of those opportunities. We will also discuss some of the unique features of television communication and give a brief preview of this book.

Chapter 2 addresses personal considerations that face all television communicators: objectives, contacts, and relationships that are involved in getting your message across.

In later chapters we will consider content and structure in television messages, tour a television studio and note the kinds of equipment necessary for television communication, and discuss the presentational, interview, and ethical features common in the personal use of television. When you have finished this book, you will be more aware of your opportunities to use television and of the skills necessary to communicate effectively on television.

PART
ONE

1. THE LANGUAGE OF TELEVISION

As consumers of television we are well aware of its presence in our daily life. Americans have more television sets than telephones, automobiles, refrigerators, or bathtubs, and recent high school graduates have spent more hours watching television than they have spent in school. Television has become so central in contemporary human affairs that Alistair Cooke has called it "the language of the twentieth century." It is a language we must all understand and use if we are to be relevant in our own time. The purpose of this book is to examine the effective use of television in personal and professional communications.

We are writing this book for two reasons. First, the experience of being on television has become available to people from all walks of life, not just professional broadcasters. Second, television communication is not the same as traditional face-to-face communication—it requires special skills. In this chapter we discuss television as an increasingly common medium of human exchange and we illustrate some of its unique features.

Figure 1.1

Today's compact, mobile equipment makes it possible
for people from all walks of life to take advantage of
television—both behind and in front of the camera.

INDIVIDUAL USES OF TELEVISION

We are moving into a new age, an age of personalized mass communication. We see evidence of this new era in increasing individual uses of television.

Broadcast Outlets

We have all experienced television communication as recipients, but until recently active participation has been closed to individuals. Things are changing. Individual use of television has become an important development in mass communications; indeed, there is a high proba-

bility that at some point in your life, either by chance or design, you are
going to find yourself in front of a television camera as part of your normal communication activity. Professionals, as well as lay citizens, will
be moving from a position of simply watching television to being active
participants.

Technological advances in the production, transmission, and distri-
bution of televised messages are partly responsible for the increased
likelihood that we will all appear on television. These advances have led
to new channel options. During the 1940s, the word *television* described
a handful of stations transmitting the same programs to a general audience. But as television became more popular, the number of stations
aimed at a more localized and specific audience increased dramatically.
By 1980 there were 800 commercial stations beaming programs into
millions of homes.

Public television, with its 300 stations, quickly joined commercial
television in our living rooms and classrooms. The advent of cable and
satellite systems is bringing yet another rapid increase in the number of
available channels. Many cities already offer their residents 50 channels
to choose from, some catering almost completely to special interest
groups. For example, there are channels devoted exclusively to news, to
women, children, blacks, Jews, senior citizens, Christians, Hispanics,
Asians, devotees of sports and culture, and fitness enthusiasts. With its
multi-channel systems, cable provides prospects for even further expan-
sion; one new television set has a 170-channel capacity.

Satellites are yet another stimulus for the individual use of television. *Television/Radio Age* has noted that "a program distributor
need only buy time on a satellite, presto, he has a nationwide cable
TV network. . . . [H]e can selectively feed any group of systems he
chooses."[1]

The Federal Communications Commission (FCC) in 1982 adopted a
plan that will add yet another 4,000 television stations. By licensing
what are called "low-power systems" (a broadcasting range of only ten to
fifteen miles), the Commission set in motion a plan that would allow
anyone with approximately $100,000 and a license to open a television
station. Local and specialized programming will become even more prevalent as these new outlets try to satisfy their viewers.

And as more programs are broadcast, more people are needed to
take part in these broadcasts. Teachers, political leaders, business persons, and members of the community in general are being asked or are
volunteering to appear on television. All of them will need to develop
television skills.

Private Video

Television's new impact on daily communication does not stop with commercial, educational, and cable outlets. Inexpensive, portable video equipment enables people to record and play back personalized television programs. In his book *The Executive's Guide to TV and Radio Appearances,* Michael Bland suggests that a private studio "can be established for the cost of a month's salary of an average chief executive."[2] Many companies, organizations, and schools are finding it beneficial and profitable to produce their own programs. In Akron, Ohio, for example, the city hospital runs a health education channel that is used by both staff and patients to transmit important information.

There are now over 10 million private, portable video units in existence. Clearly the electronic innovations of the past decade have enabled more and more people to appear on television. Everyone has a wide range of choice in both sending and receiving television messages.

THE PEOPLE ON TELEVISION

Business People

The business community was quick to realize the value of television as an advertising medium. Our television screens are filled with images of Eastern Air Lines chairman Frank Borman boasting of a number one ranking in passenger boarding, Joseph Schlitz Brewing boss Frank Sellinger urging beer lovers to "taste my Schlitz," Victor Kiam II recalling his wife's gift of a Remington Micro Screen shaver and adding, "I was so impressed, I bought the company," and Chrysler's Lee Iacocca planting himself on an assembly line and growling, "If you can find a better car, buy it."

An executive starring in a commercial illustrates but one example of how business makes use of television. AT&T, for instance, offers a two-way **teleconferencing** service that enables business people to conduct face-to-face meetings via a transcontinental video network that puts all the participants "on television" at the same time. Full-page ads showing executives on television now appear in *Time* and *Newsweek* with the following caption: "Getting together by satellite—the world's largest privately owned earth station network lets you hold video-conference meetings at hundreds of Holiday Inn hotels at the same time." In addition, many companies such as Xerox, Corning, New England Mutual Life Insurance, and Holiday Inn Corporation use television for training, research, employee relations, and the exchanging of in-house information. Some organizations even have elaborate systems that can be called "mini-private networks."[3]

Current technology is likely to involve executives and salespersons in some of the following scenarios: A company vice-president argues her firm's philosophy on nuclear waste on a *60 Minutes* segment; a member of an organization's marketing department videotapes a lecture for his staff on some new products; the members of an international division hold a teleconference with their colleagues 3,000 miles away; the president of a company videotapes a welcoming speech for new employees. There are even systems that allow a company to conduct employment, evaluation, and problem-solving interviews via television.

Teachers

Educators are well aware of how effective television can be as a teaching aid. High school and college teachers are using closed-circuit systems to teach large groups of students; they are also making specific videotapes to supplement their regular classroom activities. In addition, instruction is now moving beyond the confines of individual campuses. The Public Broadcasting Service, for example, offers courses for credit via 206 television stations. New programs on cooking, dog training, health, leisure time, money management, and the like are introduced regularly.

The Stanford Instructional Television Network (SITN), through the Stanford University School of Engineering, provides graduate education to several thousand professional engineers, managers, and staff from a hundred San Francisco Bay Area companies and research institutions. This interactive educational system, with one-way and two-way audio, broadcasts twelve hours a day on four channels allocated by the FCC. It offers eighty courses in business administration, management development, supervision, and computer science, all taught by professors speaking the language of the twentieth century.

Educators are also realizing the need for their students to learn the skills of television communication. In Mar Vista, California, for example, 10- to 18-year-olds are studying the art of being natural in front of a camera.

Preachers

Bible study, mass, and gospel singing are available on television any Sunday morning in America. Jerry Falwell and Oral Roberts are only two of many people ministering through cable, satellite, and commercial television outlets. Many religious speakers are also using video cassettes as a way of reaching audiences who can't attend services. Clearly, mastering the language of television is an important part of contemporary religious training.

Medical Personnel

Television is becoming a major language of the medical profession. Doctors are often provided the opportunity to talk to television reporters about matters of health. More importantly, the traditional operating theatre (an operating room designed for an audience) is giving way to operating television studios where doctors, sometimes separated by thousands of miles, share in significant operations. A new Hospital Satellite Network will soon be providing a communication outlet for doctors, nurses, and hospital administrators, as well as a million patients in 600 hospitals. Here again, people who have never been part of television communication will find themselves in front of the camera.

Judges, Lawyers, Defendants

One of the most controversial uses of television is in the courtroom. It began in 1954 with the murder trial of Sam Sheppard, a young surgeon accused of killing his wife. When Judge Edward Blythin allowed the press free access to the courtroom, their presence became an issue itself. Sheppard's conviction was overturned because the press made a circus of the trial. It took seventeen years before a civil case (*McCall* v. *Clemens*) became the first to be videotaped and shown to a jury.

In 1981 the United States Supreme Court ruled that the presence of television reporters in the courtroom did not automatically interfere with the defendant's rights to a fair trial. Twenty-seven states now allow television cameras in the courtroom and the list is likely to grow. The Supreme Court decision, combined with a 1982 American Bar Association ruling that concurred with that decision, means that lawyers, defendants, witnesses, and judges are now appearing and communicating before the camera.

Videotape is also being used to record confessions and to present relevant evidence. In Nevada, prisoners are arraigned via television. Defendants and lawyers untrained in the medium of television might well find themselves at a disadvantage. As a member of the Los Angele Public Defender's Office recently noted, "Because of cameras in the courtroom, a different method of speaking will be needed."[4]

Figure 1.2
Politicians have long recognized the importance of
television to their profession.

Many law schools are already adapting their curricula to meet this new need. The staff of the McGeorge School of Law in Sacramento, California, includes a "court technician" who operates remote-controlled cameras for videotaping courtroom proceedings that students can replay in library viewing rooms. Obviously the McGeorge School believes, as we do, that the courtroom of the future includes television communication.[5]

Politicians

Politicians have long recognized the importance of television to their profession. They have used it as a means of getting and staying elected, and for gaining support for their proposals. The House of Representatives now has gavel-to-gavel coverage that can reach over 7.5 million homes.

National politicians aren't the only ones who are appearing on television. A recent article in the *San Diego Union* headlined "Council Members Become TV Stars in Oceanside" announced that city council meetings were going to be aired on the city's two franchised cable television systems.

It is not only elected officials who must learn to use television. Kingman Brewster, on his retirement as ambassador to Great Britain, suggested that ambassadors must know how to use the skills of television communication as part of their appointment and assignment. Whether on the local, state, national, or international level, people involved with public policy are going to be involved with television.

THE UNIQUE FEATURES OF TELEVISION COMMUNICATION

The language of the twentieth century is becoming ubiquitous. To understand that language, it is necessary to consider how television communication differs from ordinary face-to-face communication. From our experience we have isolated eight features unique to television communication. The following brief outline of these features will prepare you for more in-depth discussions throughout this book.

1. Distractions

Television viewers face a number of distractions as they watch television, but they can control many of them. If someone is talking while they are trying to listen, they can ask the person to be still, or they can turn up the volume. But for the television *speaker,* distractions are unavoidable: microphones and cameras zooming from place to place, technicians attending to equipment, producers and directors giving cues and signals. Being able to concentrate and look relaxed amid this activity is often what separates the advanced television communicator from the novice.

2. Heterogeneous Audiences

Although some video presentations (company programs, training films, classroom instruction, and some cable programs) are aimed at very specialized audiences, the audience for television is usually more heterogeneous (varied in outlook and demographic composition) than in other forms of communication. The term *mass media* serves to underscore the point that you seldom have complete control over who will watch you—unless, of course, you own all the equipment and guard the on–off switch.

3. Mediated Communication

Television is a *mediated* event. No matter how informal or intimate the conversation might be, a boundary still exists between speaker and listener: The electronic components of television keep you and your audience apart. This simple idea must be kept in mind as you prepare and present your television message.

4. Time Constraints

A banquet speaker can smile at the audience and announce that he or she has just a few more things to add. And normal conversation is affected by time limits only in a general way. But when you appear on television, whether on a commercial, educational, or cable network, you must always adjust to the clock. Time is even an issue when using videotape in a private presentation. Once the tape runs out, you are off the screen—whether you are finished or not.

5. Collaboration

In most of your interactions, you need no intervening party. You are on your own as you establish and maintain your links with others. When communicating on television, however, you are generally involved in a collaborative effort. Before you can be seen or heard you use the time, energy, and resources of other people. Even the finest hand-held units are best operated by pairs or groups of people. And as you might guess, the more elaborate the program, the more people you need to operate the equipment and cooperate in the presentation. The collaborative aspects of television will be discussed throughout this work.

6. Action

Television, for a host of reasons, thrives on action. The ease with which viewers yield to distractions and the fact that most people were introduced to television as an entertainment medium both contribute to an emphasis on action. You will notice as you watch television that most programs change camera shots quite often, and that they employ a variety of visual effects. These two activities are not by chance—television obtains and holds attention mostly by action.

7. Control

Because television is an electronic medium and involves a collaborative effort, how the message appears to a viewer can be controlled and manipulated. By means of audio techniques (tone, volume, pitch) and visual techniques (changes in size, color, shape), your presentation can be altered. Editing devices can also affect how you appear. Learning about television techniques and devices will enable you to enhance your presentation. By working with the directors, engineers, and camera and audio personnel, you can add to the impact of your message.

8. Power

There is a power associated with being on television that is not found in most other communication situations. Viewers have assumed that to be on television, you have to be "important" and/or have the money necessary to produce your own program. The aura of importance and power often adds to the speaker's credibility.

Notice how many times you listen to a person on a talk show and find yourself responding differently than if you were talking to that person informally. Television communication is powerful! Be careful; a lot of people may be watching. A guest on a national talk show recently suggested that powdered vitamin C was better for you than tablets. In three days most health food stores were completely sold out of powdered vitamin C. Perhaps one of the most vivid examples of the power of television occurred during the 1968 Democratic convention, when anti-war demonstrators shouted "The whole world's watching!" as they confronted the Chicago police. They knew that what is said and done on television may profoundly affect your future and the future of your viewers.

OUTLINE OF BOOK

We have divided this book into six sections that cover what we feel to be the significant factors of skillful television communication. We have also included an overview that summarizes the main themes of the book and touches on some ethical and philosophical issues that must be examined by anyone who uses television. What follows is a brief description of the major parts and chapters.

Television and Human Affairs

Television speakers are the central concern of this book and the focal point of Part One. In the first chapter of this section we looked at some of the factors that have made television so much a part of our private and professional lives. We also discussed how this medium of human exchange differs from normal face-to-face interaction.

In Chapter 2 we will continue the discussion of personalizing television by describing how someone about to appear on television must (1) identify objectives, (2) understand viewers, and (3) recognize the various forms of relationships possible in television communication.

Television Content

Television is commonly thought to lack substance. In Part Two we illustrate the fact that television has and demands as much substance as any other medium of human communication. For example, we see evidence (Chapter 3) and reason (Chapter 4) as important substantive concerns in the use of television.

Structure in Television Messages

Television is characterized not only by content and substance, but also by a high degree of organization. In Part Three we point out that television messages are not random and aimless. We will discuss general and specific means of organizing television messages in Chapters 5 and 6.

The Television Studio

In Part Four we note that a number of studio options of varying complexity exist for anyone using television. A home studio, for example, is obviously not as complex as the production facilities at NBC. Yet all facilities share some similarities. They have a common language (Chapter 7), cameras and microphones (Chapter 8), and other equipment (Chapter 9), that you should be familiar with if you use or intend to use television.

Television Presentation

The human, substantive, organizational, and studio variables of television communication are all prelude to delivery. Delivering your message moves your ideas into the minds of others. Hence, the way you present yourself and your thoughts is the subject of Part Five. There are countless examples, including the famous Nixon–Kennedy presidential television debates, where muffed delivery, poor animation, a dull voice, and improper makeup have influenced the outcome of the communication event. We will therefore discuss both the visual (Chapter 10) and auditory (Chapter 11) dimensions of television delivery.

Television Interviews

It's impossible to predict every occasion you may have for television communication. However, some situations will occur more often than others. Interviews, for example, are a very common form of television communication, and it is important for anyone planning to use television to feel comfortable in press, host, mediated, or employment interviews. In Part Six we will examine how to prepare (Chapter 12) and participate in (Chapter 13) these types of television encounters.

Issues in the Use of Television

There is a tendency to perceive television as an "it," something that more or less just happens. In the overview we discuss television as a medium of human communication involving decision-making. We examine some of the ethical issues underlying the use of television and how those issues demand decisions by people using television as their medium of expression.

Each section of this book ends with a review containing a summary of the section, evaluation forms that can be used to measure your understanding and use of television, and a list of references that may enhance your understanding and use of television. We cannot guarantee that this book will make you a successful television speaker. But we do believe that the skills and issues discussed in this book can move you in the right direction, can assist you in communicating effectively on television.

2. PERSONAL CONSIDERATIONS IN TELEVISION COMMUNICATION

As we use television more in our everyday affairs, the medium becomes personalized. That is to say, although it does possess those unique features outlined in Chapter 1, it also mirrors many aspects of face-to-face interaction. Three of these characteristics—objectives, contacts, and relationships—are important to anyone concerned with improving his or her television presentation.

PERSONAL OBJECTIVES

Whether we care to admit it or not, communication is always motivated by some sense of objective: We want something when we talk. In discussing personal objectives in television communication, we will first offer a general definition of what we mean by *objectives*. Second, we will discuss and classify what we call *programming objectives*. Third, we will talk about the importance of meshing personal and programming objectives in your television communications.

General Definition

Traditional studies of communication suggest that human expression is generated by three principal objectives: information, entertainment, and persuasion.

We associate **information objectives** with such terms as *data, knowledge, wisdom,* and *reason;* Mr. Spock, of the *Star Trek* series, personified what we would call information objectives. We associate **entertainment objectives** with such terms as *sensation, enjoyment,* and *pleasure;* when we sing "Happy Birthday" to our friends or send them singing telegrams, we are revealing our entertainment objectives. We associate **persuasion objectives** with such terms as *conviction* and *belief;* when we argue politics or religion, we are revealing persuasion objectives.

Personal use of television clearly involves these three objectives. For example, one of the authors is developing a video connection between two university systems separated by 400 miles. The primary objective is to exchange information; a secondary objective is the pleasure of collegial interchange; and a third objective is to persuade the people involved to engage in co-taught video courses, enhancing the course offerings of both institutions.

Knowing your personal objectives is important, since they will not only dictate the material, tone, and feel of your television presentation, but will also need to be compatible with your programming opportunities.

Programming Objectives

Electronic components do not have objectives; people do. Television programming reflects the same objectives as private conversations. News and educational programs in general reflect information objectives. The soaps and most prime-time programs are intended to entertain. And commercials and political and religious addresses try to persuade.

However, although most programs emphasize one objective or another, every television communication entails a bit of each objective. That a communication may have several objectives has led us to propose a classification system of television programming. Since any communication situation can be categorized according to primary, secondary, and tertiary objectives, such categorization results in six possible configurations of information, persuasion, and entertainment objectives (see table).[6]

SIX CONFIGURATIONS OF TELEVISION PROGRAMMING

Configuration number	1	2	3	4	5	6
Primary objective	I	I	E	E	P	P
Secondary objective	E	P	I	P	I	E
Tertiary objective	P	E	P	I	E	I

Key: I = Information; E = Entertainment; P = Persuasion.

The first configuration, for example, illustrates a message that emphasizes an information objective. Its secondary objective is to entertain, and its third is to persuade. This configuration fits our perception of the average anchor person—someone whose first obligation is to inform, but who might also engage in entertainment and persuasion.

The configurations broadly classify television programming and suggest the options available to anyone using television. For example, an East Coast company is now packaging what it calls "infomercials" for cable television. The first avowed objective of the infomercial is to inform the viewer of the company's products and standards; the second is to encourage purchase of the company's products. Given the need to maintain interest and attention, we would suppose that entertainment is a third objective of the infomercial. In short, we would categorize the infomercial as a type 2 configuration.

If you have complete control over the content of your presentation, as well as complete control over the equipment, the people operating the equipment, the sponsors of the program, and the channel of programming, then you may not have to think about how your objectives fit with your programming opportunities. Most situations involving television communication are not so individually controlled, however. The six configurations help you estimate how well your objectives fit with the opportunities you have to use television.

Meshing Personal and Programming Objectives

We noted earlier that television is a collaborative medium. The interactive nature of television is nowhere more apparent than in objectives. In preparing for a television presentation, you are well advised to consider your personal objectives relative to the program being produced. When personal and programming objectives clash, confusion, protest, and disaster can result.

Many skits on *Saturday Night Live* use such confusion as the basis for their humor. A newscaster on the *SNL* news segment introduces a guest commentator who, we are told, will discuss a certain topic. Then the commentator, after merely a few words about the announced subject, becomes sidetracked by a particular detail. Soon the entire presentation becomes a hilarious, frenetic personal vendetta instead of a reasoned, calm discourse.

A clash in objectives can also be a serious matter. When Marlon Brando and Vanessa Redgrave injected political statements into the frilly atmosphere of Academy Awards presentations, they provoked anger and protest.

Far more disturbing is the story of a newscaster who committed suicide on camera while protesting the emphasis on blood and guts in news coverage.[7] Daniel Schorr, in reviewing the incident, suggested that the act was the result of tensions between personal and programming objectives.[8] While other problems no doubt contributed to the tragedy, the story does provide an extreme example of real-life conflicts faced by many people in television.

Understanding your objectives relative to those of the program you appear on can be crucial. Recently a Las Vegas shopping mall established a video job center where anyone can air his or her qualifications for employment. Most of the applicants try to convey their skills and desirability; that is, they are informational and persuasive. Some miss the point, however, and joke their way through the presentation, failing to mesh personal with program objectives.

Your effectiveness on television depends on how well you can mesh your own objectives with those of the program you are a part of. Personal contacts and personal relationships are also important in communicating effectively on television.

PERSONAL CONTACT IN TELEVISION COMMUNICATION

One of the strangest discoveries we have made in teaching television communication is that novices often fail to think about their audience. Television communication is a two-way process; however, not all speakers seem aware of the fact. There are some who, since they have the camera's eye on them, assume that they are the more important half of the communication equation. Such speakers do not make contact with their viewers. On the other hand, there are speakers who will do anything for an audience, like a character from John Irving's novel *The Hotel New Hampshire* who was "willing to murder and maim—not for a cause, which would be stupid enough, but for an audience."[9]

The position taken in this book is that the speakers and viewers of a television message are equal in importance. Although speakers must deal with personal objectives, they must understand (1) the people they contact with television and (2) how audience objectives may affect a speaker.

The People You Contact

A television audience is not personal in the sense of close physical presence. And yet a television speaker can develop close personal ties with an audience by sharing personal information. We can't tell you the names or the specific traits of your television audience, but we can tell you about the kinds of information that will help you develop personal contact with your audience. In personalizing television presentations, it's important to understand audience **kinship, composition,** and **intensity.**

KINSHIP Kinship in television audiences can be defined by **homogeneity** or **heterogeneity.** A homogeneous audience is one that shares characteristics. For example, we might assume that the audience of a cable television system established for the retirement community of Sun City is related by age range. However, there is also heterogeneity among Sun City residents: differences of income, political views, and so on.

In preparing for a television audience, a speaker must recognize the homogeneity as well as the heterogeneity of the audience. Such recognition comes from personal experience as well as observation of the specific composition of audiences.

COMPOSITION The study of audience composition is known as **demographics.** The following are some of the more common demographic concerns that you might think about as you begin to tailor your message to your audience.

Age	Religion
Gender	Occupation
Reference groups or clubs	Education
Power	Social status
Affiliations	Politics
Size	Geographic location
Economic status	Cultural background

Knowing the demographic features of your audience will help you personalize your television message.

INTENSITY   Audiences, just like individuals, have varying levels of intensity. The degree to which you establish personal contact with your audience depends on intensity of audience interest and involvement. H. L. Hollingworth, in *The Psychology of the Audience,* suggests classifying audiences as "passive," "concerted," or "organized" on the basis of their intensity of interest and involvement.[10]

A **passive audience** is an audience that does not just drop in, an audience that has some homogeneity and some interest in the speaker or the presentation. A **concerted audience** demonstrates a good deal of homogeneity and an active interest in the speaker or the presentation. Fans of programs like *Dynasty* are examples of concerted audiences. An **organized audience** is composed of people who have interest in the program or the speaker and who have organized themselves in the pursuit of their interest. Consumer interest groups and political clubs are examples of organized audiences.

Several types of audience might watch any given presentation. For example, one author was once the host of a fourteen-week series called "Media Watch," a two-minute segment of the six o'clock news offering critical reviews of television, radio, and print media.

The viewers of the evening news were a passive audience. According to letters and ratings, the audience tuned into the program because the station had the most popular news anchor in town. "Media Watch," though incidental, was a part of the overall presentation. "Media Watch" also had a concerted audience: the people who worked in media. The segment took a critical, fairly aggressive stance. Phone calls demonstrated that media representatives kept an eye on it. That the segment also had an organized audience became clear when one newspaper publisher became quite irate over some criticism directed at his paper. His representatives made it apparent that the program had a fan club of sorts—an organized body of viewers in pursuit of their legal interests.

Identifying the intensity of an audience, like identifying its composition and homogeneity, will affect how you prepare your presentation. For a casual audience, you have to work hard at getting and maintaining attention. For an organized audience, depth becomes more important than gaining attention.

Audience intensity may be gauged and prepared for at three distinct points in a television presentation. First, before you put a presentation together you can predict the intensity of the target audience by closely studying demographic information. Second, intensity can be determined by a pilot program screened for a group that is representative of the target audience. Finally, once a program is aired, reviews, letters, and surveys reveal whether a speaker has correctly determined and suited the intensity of the audience.

The Effects of Contact

Having information about an audience does not automatically lead to successful communication. Once the information is gathered, a speaker must draw conclusions from it and translate those conclusions into effective programming choices. An adaptive speaker changes with audience analysis. Huber W. Ellingsworth and Theodore Clevenger, Jr., have suggested four effects that audience information may have on a speaker: restraint, constraint, options, and opportunities.[11]

The characteristics of an audience establish **restraints,** what cannot be said. Certain prime-time material may not be acceptable in programming for children. In television, as in all communication, what and how a speaker communicates is restrained by the people being addressed.

Audience characteristics also establish **constraints,** what must be said. For example, terms that are not known to an audience must be defined; a speaker not known to an audience must be introduced.

Restraints and constraints on a speaker would seem to delimit a speaker's repertoire. However, as Ellingsworth and Clevenger note, the characteristics of an audience "provide criteria for selecting among alternate forms of the message." There is always more than one way to say what one wishes to say. Between what cannot be said and what must be said, a speaker is left with a universe of **options.** Analysis of an audience reveals options as well as restraints and constraints.

Ellingsworth and Clevenger also note that audience characteristics may "suggest **opportunities** for producing special effects." Special effects are generally viewed as technical concerns, but they are mentioned here because the development and success of special effects depends, in part, on the audience. Audience analysis can help determine what will be special to an audience and what will have effect. Knowing your audience could help you decide if you should use a single photograph as a special effect or if you need a short film to make the point. For example, try to imagine the adjustments you would have to make if you were a computer expert speaking to your peers at seven o'clock, then to a lay audience at eight. This process of reflection is at the core of audience analysis.

PERSONAL RELATIONSHIPS IN TELEVISION COMMUNICATION

There are conventions and rituals involved in communication. The various personal relationships possible between speakers and listeners can be codified into four forms, all of which are possible in television communication.

Intrapersonal communication is self-communication. **Interpersonal communication** occurs when two or a few people are engaged in more or less intimate conversation. **Group communication** involves two to fifty people, with the possibility of face-to-face interaction. **Public communication** involves a large audience with little chance of face-to-face interaction between participants.

Intrapersonal Communication

Intrapersonal communication is not a common television form, but it does exist. Televised versions of *Hamlet* present the soliloquies in much the same way this intrapersonal form has been portrayed on the stage— a person alone, functioning as both source and receiver. The intrapersonal poetry of Emily Dickinson has also been dramatized in the medium of television. You may never want to use television for *your* intrapersonal conversations, but you might want to use it to portray the intrapersonal conversations of others. There is no reason to assume that we will not, one day, watch as the camera sneaks into Mrs. Olson's kitchen to overhear her intrapersonal mutterings about the merits of her particular brand of coffee.

Interpersonal Communication

The study of interpersonal communication focuses on those things that we do and say one to one. Increased access to television, as discussed in Chapter 1, leads to increased opportunity for interpersonal television communications. And, as we will soon point out, television has from its inception reflected interpersonal dialogue.

The degree to which television has become a part of interpersonal address is well documented in *Inter/Media,* edited by Gary Gumpert and Robert Cathcart. In detailing the nexus of media and interpersonal communication, Gumpert and Cathcart say that "it is misleading to study interpersonal communication and pretend that media do not influence the phenomenon. It is equally misleading to represent the media world as one disconnected from our interpersonal relations."[12] Television equipment is not only accessible, it is becoming necessary in many legal, economic, and social situations.

Figure 2.1

*Television can be as personal as the participants
are willing to make it. Consider how much interest
would be lost if this interview had been conducted in
a neutral studio environment.*

Job interviews, court arraignments, and many other one-to-one situations are now possible through the medium of television. Home systems of video production make it possible for individuals to send tapes
like letters. In the future, love letters may become love tapes.

Even in the past, television always manifested some signs of interpersonal communication. There was a closeness and commitment between Edward R. Murrow and his viewers. Johnny Carson often remarks on the fact that he is entering the bedrooms of America, and he
commonly engages in interpersonal communication with both his studio
and home audiences. In the 1970s, news programs began to exhibit an
increasing interpersonality. Every anchor person suddenly seemed to
love every member of the news team, and audiences became privy to
their interpersonal interactions.

Commercials have been a steady reflector of interpersonal communications, regularly taking television viewers into personal space. We've
watched and listened as Madge the manicurist interpersonally sells her

brand of dishwashing liquid. Cigarette commercials (before they were banned) tended to feature a man and a woman meeting in open but private spaces, selling one another on taste, smoothness, and interpersonal pleasure.

In interpersonal communication, as in intrapersonal communication, you have to consider how close to home you want to bring a camera, and, possibly, an audience. There is a fine line between what we are willing to talk about with loved ones and what we are willing to expose to strangers. Anyone preparing to use television should consider that line before engaging in interpersonal television. (Interviewing, one of the more common forms of interpersonal television, will be discussed at greater length in Part Six.)

Group Communication

Television is generally a group effort. News teams are an example of group interaction on television. The reporters in the field have their stories channeled to the anchor people who, in turn, may question the reporters. In an important story, numerous reporters may be linked together, along with group leaders (anchors).

The group interaction involved in the evening news is possible outside broadcast television—for example, in video conferencing, still in its beginning stages. Universities, large businesses, and government agencies engage in group communication through two-way video stations. The current research in fiber optics and laser communications suggests that the number of television outlets available for group communication can increase far beyond present levels.

Public Communication

Public communication involves a single speaker and a formality not generally present in group and interpersonal communication. In its traditional form it demands that the audience be assembled in one spot and that the speaker stand before the audience, in an elevated position.

In 1981 a Cuban official was to deliver an address to the United Nations, but he was denied entry to the United States. Undaunted, the official videotaped his address, which was then replayed to the assembly. Videotape makes it possible for a speaker and his public to meet, even though separated by geographic and political boundaries.

American presidents commonly use television for public communication. They tend to work from a prepared address, to speak uninterruptedly, and are formal in both manner and organization. On the eve of his 1980 election, Ronald Reagan addressed various audiences across America through the use of pretaped public speeches.

Figure 2.2
Television often reflects group communication.
(Photography by Scott Highton, courtesy of Over
Easy/KQED.)

Examples of public address in videotape form are becoming in-creasingly common. Religious, political, and educational leaders have, with videotape, the opportunity to meet their public in a way that cir-cumvents the rigors and expenses of physical travel.

Public communication can be complex. For example, many of Presi-dent Reagan's congressional addresses have been televised, leading to some question as to who the primary audience really was. Such an ad-dress is tricky to formulate, since to recognize the removed (home) audi-ence overtly could lead to a failure with the immediate (congressional) audience. It could be like looking over someone's shoulder while talking to her at a party—a display of bad manners.

A television speaker must be careful to keep the nature of public communication clearly in mind. A public is composed of people who are not as close to the speaker as the speaker's loved ones. A public is not a small group of people capable of face-to-face interaction. A speaker and his public may share certain values and experiences, but becoming too interpersonal in public address can be a mistake.

When the situation, audience, and speaker encourage the use of a public address form, a television speaker has two choices: to use tele-vision as the channel for address, or to use television as a mirror of the address. As a channel, television allows fairly direct contact with the audience. As a mirror, television allows the audience some distance from the event and may enhance credibility by generating the sense of having overheard the address. For example, if a speech delivered by the president of a company to her senior staff is put on tape and played back to the stockholders, the stockholders might feel as if they were "listening in" to an earlier event.

SUMMARY

Understanding the various forms of communication is a matter of sense and sensitivity. What is your best form of interaction? How does that form relate to the form expected by the audience? Is the situation conducive to your chosen form of speaking? Answering these questions is prologue to communicating effectively with television.

The treatment of forms in this chapter has been brief. Observing form in everyday communication and observing form in television should enhance a speaker's ability to choose the appropriate form for his or her television presentations. The sources footnoted in this chapter may also assist a speaker in making this decision.

Failure to understand these forms can lead to failure in communication. An example of such failure occurred in a recent interview between a university president and a local reporter during halftime of a nationally televised basketball game. The situation was common enough—as were the errors made.

The reporter, after a brief prologue in which he identified himself, the station, and the interviewee, moved back to the president and asked him the first question. But the reporter couldn't seem to decide who he was talking with; he kept turning, as the president spoke, to face the television audience. The president, obviously unpracticed, followed the lead of the reporter.

The choices were obvious. Both parties to the interview could have maintained an interpersonal dialogue, treating the camera like a silent party to the conversation, a person who would nod and follow, but not participate. Or they could have simply chosen to be public speakers and done their bit facing the camera. Instead, they vacillated, never quite getting their interaction in sync.

Successful television presentations begin with some sense of personal objective, progress to recognition of the other people involved in the communication act, and end in the development of some personal relationship between the speaker and those being addressed.

PART
ONE

TELEVISION AND HUMAN AFFAIRS
REVIEW

In Chapter 1 we documented the expanding use of television, pointing out that increased access makes television more personal and makes it necessary for each of us to focus and adapt our communication skills to the language of television. We also discussed some of the unique features of television communication that require special attention.

In Chapter 2 we discussed the personal considerations of effective television communication. Understanding your personal and program objectives and how they mesh is a crucial first step in preparing your presentation.

It is important to know something about the people you may contact with your television message. Understanding personal objectives and your audience enables you to develop the relationship best suited to your television presentation.

Being aware of options in television communication and the personal considerations that go with such options are only beginning steps in communicating effectively on television. Content and organization are equally important in television presentations; these subjects will be covered in Part Two.

RESOURCES

Notes

1. As noted by Alvin Toffler in *The Third Wave* (New York: Morrow, 1980), p. 180.
2. Michael Bland, *The Executive's Guide to TV and Radio Appearances* (New York: Van Nostrand Reinhold, 1979), p. 91.
3. John Quick and Herbert Wolff, *Small-Studio Video Tape Production,* 2nd ed. (Reading, Mass.: Addison-Wesley, 1976), pp. 9–10.
4. Herbert Barish, "Cameras in the Courtroom: Theory and Practice," Speech Communication Association Convention, Los Angeles, Calif., November 1981.
5. For further information on "The Courtroom of the Future," contact McGeorge School of Law, 3200 Fifth Ave., Sacramento, Calif. 95817.
6. For further discussion of classifying television programming by objectives, see "Human Motive in Television Programming" by Evan Blythin and Larry Samovar (paper delivered at the Western States Communication Convention, Denver, Colo., February 1982).
7. "Talk Show Hostess Dies," *New York Times,* 16 July 1974, p. 23.
8. Daniel Schorr, " 'Network' News," *Rolling Stone,* 16 December 1976, p. 41.
9. John Irving, *The Hotel New Hampshire* (New York: E. P. Dutton, 1981), p. 314.
10. H. L. Hollingworth, *The Psychology of the Audience* (New York: American Book Co., 1935), pp. 19–32.
11. Huber W. Ellingsworth and Theodore Clevenger, Jr., *Speech and Social Action* (Englewood Cliffs, N.J.: Prentice-Hall, 1967), pp. 111–113.
12. Gary Gumpert and Robert Cathcart, eds., *Inter/Media: Interpersonal Communication in a Media World* (New York: Oxford University Press, 1979), p. v.

Recommended Readings

INTRAPERSONAL COMMUNICATION

AUSTIN-LETT, GENELLE, and JAN SPRAGUE. *Talk to Yourself.* Boston: Houghton Mifflin, 1976.

CARR, JACQUELYN B. *Communicating With Myself: A Journal.* Reading, Mass.: Benjamin/Cummings, 1979.

DEL POLITO, CAROLYN M. *Intrapersonal Communication*. Reading, Mass.: Cummings, 1977.

HAMACHEK, DON E. *Encounters with the Self*. New York: Holt, Rinehart and Winston, 1971.

PRATHER, HUGH. *Notes to Myself*. Lafayette, Calif.: Real People Press, 1970.

INTERPERSONAL COMMUNICATION

BARNLUND, DEAN. *Interpersonal Communication: Survey and Studies*. Boston: Houghton Mifflin, 1968.

GUMPERT, GARY, and ROBERT CATHCART, eds. *Inter/Media: Interpersonal Communication in a Media World*. New York: Oxford University Press, 1979.

PEARSON, JUDY C. *Interpersonal Communication*. Glenview, Ill.: Scott, Foresman, 1983.

TRIANDIS, HARRY C. *Interpersonal Behavior*. Monterey, Calif.: Brooks/Cole, 1977.

VANDEMARK, JO ANN F., and PAMELA C. LETH. *Interpersonal Communication*. Menlo Park, Calif.: Cummings, 1977.

GROUP COMMUNICATION

BERTCHER, HARVEY J. *Group Participation*. Beverly Hills, Calif.: Sage, 1979.

CATHCART, ROBERT S., and LARRY A. SAMOVAR, eds. *Small Group Communication: A Reader*. 3rd ed. Dubuque, Iowa: William C. Brown, 1979.

FISHER, AUBREY. *Small Group Decision Making*. 2nd ed. New York: McGraw-Hill, 1980.

GULLEY, HALBERT E., and DALE M. LEATHERS. *Communication and Group Process*. New York: Holt, Rinehart and Winston, 1977.

MABRY, EDWARD A., and RICHARD E. BARNES. *The Dynamics of Small Group Communication*. Englewood Cliffs, N.J.: Prentice-Hall, 1980.

PUBLIC COMMUNICATION

BLANKENSHIP, JANE, and ROBERT WILHOIT. *Selected Readings in Public Speaking*. Belmont, Calif.: Dickenson, 1966.

EHNINGER, DOUGLAS; BRUCE E. GRONBECK; and ALAN H. MONROE. *Principles of Speech Communication*. 8th ed. Glenview, Ill.: Scott, Foresman, 1980.

SAMOVAR, LARRY A., and JACK MILLS. *Oral Communication: Message and Response.* 5th ed. Dubuque, Iowa: William C. Brown, 1983.

VEDERBER, RUDOLPH E. *The Challenge of Effective Speaking.* 5th ed. Belmont, Calif.: Wadsworth, 1982.

WEAVER, RICHARD L. II. *Understanding Public Communication.* Englewood Cliffs, N.J.: Prentice-Hall, 1983.

TELEVISION AND HUMAN AFFAIRS

Whether you are in front of the camera or in front of the screen, you can engage in critical activities that will improve your mastery of the language of television. As you will note, each part of this book is followed by an evaluation form, noting the material discussed in the part and presenting a rating system that allows you to evaluate your or someone else's television presentation.

For example, you can use the following form to rank how well you are prepared for the unique and personal considerations of television communication—before and after the presentation. This form is applicable in many different situations. It can be used to evaluate the performance of professionals, yourself, or friends on broadcast, closed-circuit, or home video presentations. By applying critical judgment to your practice sessions, you can become more skilled and confident in your use of the language of television.

KEY: 0 = Item does not apply
            1 = Extremely well done
            2 = Fairly well done
            3 = Moderately well done
            4 = Poorly done; needs improvement

CHAPTER 1. The Language of Television

A. Understood the unique features of television
      1. Distractions   0 1 2 3 4
      2. Heterogeneous audiences   0 1 2 3 4
      3. Mediated communication   0 1 2 3 4
      4. Time constraints   0 1 2 3 4
      5. Collaboration   0 1 2 3 4
      6. Action   0 1 2 3 4
      7. Control   0 1 2 3 4
      8. Power   0 1 2 3 4

CHAPTER 2. Personal Considerations in the Use of Television

A. Understood personal objectives (in general)   0 1 2 3 4
      1. Identified purpose to inform   0 1 2 3 4
      2. Identified purpose to entertain   0 1 2 3 4
      3. Identified purpose to persuade   0 1 2 3 4
B. Understood personal contacts (in general)   0 1 2 3 4
      1. Understood kinship relationships   0 1 2 3 4
      2. Understood audience composition 0 1 2 3 4
      3. Understood audience intensity   0 1 2 3 4

C. Understood the forms of personal relationships
   (in general)   0 1 2 3 4
       1. Understood intrapersonal forms   0 1 2 3 4
       2. Understood interpersonal forms   0 1 2 3 4
       3. Understood group forms   0 1 2 3 4
       4. Understood public address forms   0 1 2 3 4

PART TWO
TELEVISION CONTENT

Reason also is choice.

Milton

critics often claim that television lacks substance because it is aimed at entertaining and commercial ends. Television programmers often claim that television lacks substance because viewers do not want substance. We know from experience that time, commercial, and audience constraints can inhibit creation of significant content. Nevertheless, as we point out in this and the final part of this book, there *is* substance in television communication.

When you stand in front of the camera, you are expected to have something to say and to say it in a clear manner. This is the purpose of *evidence* and *reason*. They are as central and basic to a television speaker as electronic components are to a television camera.

In Chapter 3 we discuss illustration and testimony as the principal components of evidence in television. In Chapter 4 we discuss comparison, induction, and deduction as the principal components of reason in television presentations.

PART
TWO

3. EVIDENCE

When we talk, we do not just randomly toss words about, and rarely can we get away with making a statement without some form of explanation. In television, as in ordinary conversation, we support our statements in two ways. First, we illustrate *what* we mean with definitions, examples, statistics, and stories. Second, we establish *how* we know with testimony. A television speaker may not hear their questions, but a television audience, like any auditor, needs and wants to know what a speaker means and how a speaker comes to know. Illustration and testimony are both important in television.

ILLUSTRATION

We often hear that "a picture is worth a thousand words"; but it is also true that a word is worth a thousand pictures. Any one visual or verbal expression encompasses many possible meanings. Definitions, examples, statistics, and stories are some common forms of illustration.

Definitions

Definition is an attempt to clarify a verbal or visual expression. The dictionary is the most common reference for precise definition. But definition need not be formulated only from a dictionary. We all have experiences that may not fit into common language, but that doesn't mean that those experiences are indescribable. We can make up words to describe what we think to be a unique experience. We can take the words that come close to explaining what we want to explain, and then redefine them in this new context.

For example, if you were appearing on a public-access channel for senior citizens, trying to establish how grocery bills could be reduced by forming "community co-ops," you would need to define your use of the word *co-op*. You could say, "When I talk today about the forming of co-ops, I'm asking the members of a community to think about working together for a common objective."

Definition may be both verbal and visual. For example, on *Sesame Street* the letter W may be defined verbally as the twenty-third letter of the alphabet, pronounced "double-u." Visually it can be broken down into its parts—V V—and those parts put together—VV VV VV—and then placed in various contexts: **W**arn, **W**arm, **W**ind, and so on. If a term or concept needs definition, a television speaker does well to consider both visual and verbal options.

Much of what the camera does in the evening news demonstrates visual definition. First we see a general picture of the newsroom, identifying a familiar scene. Then the camera focuses on a particular person, who may transfer us to yet another camera thousands of miles away that shows us another general scene and, perhaps, some particular person or event. As the camera moves back and forth, brings us closer and takes us farther from a scene or person, it is defining that scene or person.

Foreign words and names, scientific and specialized language of any sort require definition. In mass-market television, the general rule is that words should be clear and require no definition; definitions may bog down a conversation and can lead to channel-changing and dozing. Despite this general rule, every conversation may entail some need for definition. The guidelines for definition are based on common sense.

1. Don't use obscure words when known words will do.

2. Give definitions that are fairly short and precise.

3. Present a definition after the first use of the term.

4. Don't let definitions dominate a conversation; such conversation sounds like a dictionary of the air.

You should try to know your audience well enough to know which words need definition. For example, it would be embarrassing to you and a group of psychology professors were you to define such words as *recall, retention, ego,* and *behaviorism.* A speaker should also keep in mind that definitions may be both verbal and visual. The same rules of definition that apply to verbal expression apply to visual expression. Finally, remember that definition is only a means to an idea. Too much definition becomes boring and delays full development of the idea.

Examples

An example is a specific case of a general idea. Examples may be factual or hypothetical. Like definitions, they may also be verbal or visual.

An agronomist talking to an audience of farmers about a certain kind of corn blight can illustrate the blight several ways. He can bring actual samples (which require shipping expenses and could decay), he can describe the blight verbally, and he can also show video examples of the blight process. High-quality portable video equipment makes it possible to illustrate vividly the points and situations that you want to emphasize.

Examples don't always have to be real; **hypothetical example** also has its place in television. To wit: When space exploration began, there were no television cameras in space. Once the spacecraft left the ground, television news departments were limited in their coverage. Don Hewitt, a director at CBS, grappled with the problem of illustrating space progress and came up with a remarkable hypothetical example of a satellite in space. Gary Paul Gates tells the story in *Air Time:*

> First he took an ordinary globe and attached a motor to it. Then he stretched a wire clothes hanger out in a straight line, fastened one end of the hanger to the bottom of the globe, and on the other end attached a Ping-Pong ball with tiny spikes glued on it to make it look like Sputnik. When he turned on the motor, the globe slowly turned, giving the illusion that it was the Ping-Pong ball or satellite that was rotating.[1]

When Hewitt's satellite was aired, it was accompanied by verbal definition, which made it clear that the satellite was a simulation and pointed out the features that Hewitt's satellite shared with the satellite in space.

The rules of example, like the rules of definition, are basically common sense. If the example is mundane or redundant, its effectiveness is limited. Too many examples, like too much definition, may obscure a point or lead a viewer to tune out. Visual and verbal examples should enliven as well as illustrate a point.

Facts and Figures

Facts and figures (often called **statistics**) represent example after example of a given situation or event, and do so in the briefest possible statements. In television presentations they can be both helpful and harmful.

Statistics are helpful in that they condense information. The news announcer shows us a damaged nuclear plant as an example. When the announcer then states that there are twenty-four such plants in America, the figure has obviated the need to show each plant.

Facts and figures are also impressive. They indicate that you know what you're talking about. If you are an executive being questioned by a reporter, it would aid your cause if you could quote the specific cost, location, and timetable for the construction of your firm's new factory. In any conversation, having the facts and figures lends credibility.

But facts and figures can also detract from a television address. If you rattle off too many of them, you will lose your audience. Too many facts and figures, like too many examples, become boring and easily forgettable. Notice how dull and confusing the following statistics are, when presented together: "City census figures show 15 percent of New Yorkers are black, 8 percent Puerto Rican, 11 percent Italian, 4 percent Irish. There are an estimated 1,800,000 Jews, 3,400,000 Roman Catholics, and 1,700,000 Protestants. And there are three and one-half times as many registered Democrats as Republicans." One of the reasons so many early educational talk shows failed was that the speakers didn't realize that facts and figures were driving their audiences away.

Statistics can be particularly harmful if they are wrong. In our personal conversations, we can sometimes be sloppy with our facts and figures—our friends will forgive us. In television, however, as in print, incorrect facts and figures can seriously damage your credibility. You may use some fast and loose figures in a television announcement, but remember you are on record and your critics may have a good time at your expense. If you're not certain of your facts, best not air them.

There are numerous sources for statistics: Personal experience and observation can yield hard data, and every area of study has its collectors of facts and figures. For example, as we noted earlier, demographers compile population statistics. Most businesses, government agencies, and educational organizations keep statistical records.

Like definition and example, facts and figures give meaning to a statement. They indicate scope and lend precision to an idea. As with definition and example, however, they can also be overused, can be poorly used, and can detract from the point; they should be selected carefully.

Stories

Stories can be used in various ways: They entertain, they inform, and they persuade. The effectiveness of a story depends on two factors. First, a story should reflect a common understanding or truth, one that is shared by the audience. Second, a story should fit the particular point being made.

Stories take a variety of forms. **Anecdotes** are short stories of interesting and amusing content: "Bernard Shaw was the master of the ready retort. A young woman sitting next to him at a dinner party once remarked: 'What a wonderful thing is youth!' 'Yes,' he replied, 'and what a crime to waste it on children.' " **Fables,** by using animals or people, tell a story of improbable circumstances as a means of making a point: "We all know that at times too much concern can backfire. Remember the tale of the monkey who, during a flood, wanted to help his friend the fish. So he reached down into the river and showed his concern by placing the fish on a branch of the tree." **Maxims** are pithy sayings that illustrate some basic principle. "About the time one learns how to make the most of life, most of it is gone."

As with the other forms of illustration, stories can also be detrimental to a speaker's point. An overabundance of stories can clutter a presentation and obscure rather than clarify a point. They should be chosen carefully to suit the point, the audience, and the speaker.

Illustration alone does not fully answer the questions a television audience may ask you. They expect some evidence that you know what you're talking about. In one way or another, every form of illustration bears some form of testimony.

TESTIMONY

Testimony is defined by *Webster's New Collegiate Dictionary* as "first-hand authentication." The two essential elements of testimony are closeness to the subject being discussed and credibility relative to the subject.

As we noted, definitions, examples, statistics, and stories are forms of illustration; they are also forms of testimony, and their validity is based on how close the source is to the subject and how credible the source is relative to the subject.

Personal vs. Impersonal

Testimony can be personal or impersonal. If you've had **personal experience** with the subject being discussed, you can speak as one who has credibility on the subject. When Dan Rather reported on the Russian invasion of Afghanistan in 1980, he went to Afghanistan and reported his firsthand experience. His testimony was expert testimony.[2]

Testimony can also be **impersonal.** For example, if you were examining the dangers of smoking, you would want to offer the views of the United States Surgeon General. Or if you were trying to support the assertion that prisons are cruel, you could quote the warden of the state penitentiary. "I have been affiliated with prisons for fifteen years, and the only conclusion I am sure of is that they are barbaric, savage, and brutal."

It's useful to remember that definitions, examples, statistics, and stories have sources and those sources are as important as the information itself. Sources are granted credibility when they are firsthand. Sources must also be credible; *Current Biography,* the *Dictionary of American Biography, Who's Who,* and the *Dictionary of National Biography* are examples of works designed to explain who is important and why. As we pointed out earlier, in television, as in any human communication, we are first asked to illustrate what we mean; then we are asked how we know. Establishing the firsthandedness and credibility of our materials are means of addressing the question of how we know.

Common sense is the best guide in using testimony in television. If the audience is not familiar with a source of testimony, you need to thoroughly identify the source. It is not enough for *you* to know why your expert is credible—your viewers must also know. Keep in mind that testimony, like illustration, is only a part of a whole address; testimony of all forms should remain fairly brief. Finally, purely firsthand testimony is not as good as testimony that is both firsthand and credible.

SUMMARY

Whether you are an actor, a politician, a teacher, or a gardener, your television presentation should have substance. We buttress our knowledge, beliefs, and feelings with illustration and testimony. To illustrate what we know, we offer definitions, examples, statistics, and stories. In giving testimony we strive to present firsthand, authentic experience. There might be occasions when money and time may limit the substance of television, but television is not inherently inferior to any other medium of human expression; television can carry as much information as print (maybe more). We suspect that television is as substantive as the people who use it.

We cannot stress enough the need for precision in preparing television presentations. It takes about two minutes to deliver one page of typewritten material; a half-hour program might be summarized in a fifteen-page script. That is not a lot of material to introduce, sustain, and follow through on an idea, so precision in selecting material is imperative. You may have a hundred stories to illustrate your point—deciding which story does it best, for the audience you are talking with and for the time that you have is a task to be taken seriously.

In preparing your presentation, observe the elements of content in presentations similar to yours. If you are going to be a guest on the Howard Ruff show, then dissecting current shows might tell you just how many examples are commonly given to illustrate a point. It might also reveal how different speakers define their concepts as well as give you an idea of what kind of definition the audience requires. There is a tendency to think of illustration as something visual and of testimony as something auditory, but illustration and testimony blend in the audiovisual medium of television: We may illustrate something both visually and verbally, just as we might give both visual and verbal testimony.

4. REASON

Samuel Johnson wrote, "We may take Fancy for a companion, but must follow Reason as our guide." Reason has been essential to communication throughout recorded history, and its role hasn't disappeared with the advent of television. Sound reasoning is a useful guide in successful television communication. Indeed, three forms of reasoning are particularly apparent in television: **comparison,** a rudimentary form of logic that underlies all communication, and **induction** and **deduction,** other logical processes through which our experiences are placed in reasoned perspective.

COMPARISON

Computers, which mimic human thought processes, demonstrate that there are two basic ways in which people process information. One is storage, as when illustration and testimony are recorded. The other is comparison: Material is compared and contrasted so that common categories emerge and some sense is made of what would otherwise be a barrage of experience.

Donald K. Smith, in *Man Speaking,* has noted "the possibility that the observation of similitude and difference is the essential characteristic of human thought."[3] We compare what we do not know to what we know in an attempt to understand the unknown. We differentiate one experience from another. We learn by comparison, and we make judgments through comparison.

While there are numerous forms of comparison (similes, metaphors, allegories, analogies), **metaphor** is the most often used form of comparison in the language of television.

With metaphors, we compare experiences and say, as Aristotle said, "this is that."[4] All language is metaphoric; we use metaphors daily without giving them a second thought, unless we hear an unusual one or we coin our own. We say that rivers "rage" and we talk about "living color," though we know that rivers do not get angry and color does not breathe.

In television metaphor is used to bring concepts to life. For example, one television commercial proclaims that an antacid product can "cut the mustard." Another indicates that a certain cola will "open your eyes," and a third talks about a "blue-ribbon sale." We know very well that antacid does not literally cut mustard, but the concept is clear: The antacid will supposedly get the job done. Similarly, we know that a soft drink cannot open eyes, and that you will most likely not buy blue ribbons at a blue-ribbon sale. In each case, two illustrative terms are used to extract a meaning beyond either one standing alone.

Metaphoric language may also be visual. The English comedy group Monty Python, in their movie *Monty Python and the Holy Grail,* portrays a castle under seige. At one point the beseiged start hurling objects down on their attackers. Suddenly, a cow flies over the wall, as if thrown by some giant hand. The movie audience usually responds to the image with unrestrained laughter, because the comparison of a castle's defense with a thrown cow is absurd yet somehow truthful: When your life is at stake, you're liable to throw whatever you can lay your hands on.

Although they are often helpful, metaphors can also be confusing or misleading. It is important to remember that metaphoric language deals with close approximations, not literal comparisons. Every time we use more than one illustration we are comparing things that are not exactly the same. No two grains of sand or flakes of snow are ever the same. Each comparison, however, brings us closer to a concept we are trying to convey.

INDUCTION

Induction is the process of going from the particular to the general until we feel reasonably sure that the point has been made. Television often utilizes induction: A camera may zoom in and focus on particulars, giving us a series of images, a series of examples, that may lead us to some general picture.

The process of induction is very much like the process of metaphor; the difference is primarily one of quantity. In metaphor, two separate notions are merged into one package. In induction, numerous examples may be given until the characteristics that we want to focus on are refined and precisely identified. For example, we might say metaphorically that the sea was raging. Then we might illustrate the point with pictures of forty-foot waves. With each illustration our depiction of the storm becomes more precise.

The camerawork in network sports events—scanning the scene, capturing many different points of view, with many different cameras—reveals a rigorous process of induction. From the particular shots the viewer is able to piece together a general picture of how the game is going.

Like metaphor, induction is a natural part of human thought. Most people watching the PBS series *The Ascent of Man* may not have thought that they were involved in a logical process. But as host Jacob Bronowski very carefully led his audience through a detailed history, he gave examples, definitions, statistics, and adages, and induced his way to the comforting thought that the species is indeed progressing.

Where to stop is a common question in inductive reasoning. How many examples does it take to fully demonstrate a point? In part, time supplies the answer. Most television presentations are of limited duration; the number of examples is circumscribed. Therefore each example should be well chosen.

When time allows, more than one example may be offered and the advice remains the same as for a single example: Each example should be selected with care. In theory, a point is never fully illustrated until every example of the point has been examined; but in reality, we never have enough time to examine every example.

DEDUCTION

Examples and comparison lead to a general proposition or premise. Once we've reached a general proposition, we may then move to deductive reasoning. Deduction is the movement from the general to the specific.

The process of deduction is known as the **syllogism.** One of the oldest examples of a syllogism runs as follows:

       All men are mortal.   *(major premise)*
       Socrates is a man.   *(minor premise)*
       Socrates is mortal.   *(conclusion)*

The major premise is the result of induction; example after example has proved that all men are mortal. The minor premise is illustrative and provides one example of a thought, belief, or idea. From general or particular propositions we may, like Sherlock Holmes, arrive at some conclusion not made in looking at either the major or minor premise alone.

Like induction and metaphor, deduction is used in all discourse. The sportscaster tells us that a pass will be attempted. As he was not in the huddle and has not had direct experience with what is going on, he has deductively reasoned his way to pronouncement.

If pressed or if he has the time, the announcer might explain this thinking. He might say that he watched this team hundreds of times and may give example after example of how previous pass plays resembled the one being predicted: he might have induced his way to a major premise, then deduced his way to the conclusion. He could have gone through the following process:

> *Certain positions on the field indicate a pass.*
> *This team has assumed those positions which indicate a pass.*
> *This team will pass.*

A special form of deduction, the **enthymeme,** seems particularly prevalent in television. It involves the elimination of one premise. For example, we could say that all men are mortal and draw the conclusion that Socrates is mortal without stating the minor premise (that Socrates is a man).

Candiss Baksa, in researching the logical structure of television presentations, found enthymemes to be ubiquitous. In one representative example, a supermarket commercial for meat products, the video portrayed a butcher at work serving cheerful-looking customers. The portrayal is supported by a voice-over telling viewers that the customers are happy. The verbal and the visual messages establish a major premise: The customers are lucky. The voice-over also supplies a conclusion for the viewers by telling them that the consideration shown to customers "makes it lucky for you." What is not said is a minor premise, one supplied by the viewers: "I could be a customer."[5]

The use of the enthymematic structure in commercials demonstrates its efficiency. Enthymemes take less time than the whole syllogistic process, and they require participation by the viewer, who must fill in a piece of the logic.

However, enthymemes, like metaphors, can be dangerous. The clearest danger of the enthymeme is that a speaker may foist liability for their message onto the auditors. It is probably shrewd to have the audience help in the formulation of a message; but the technique is seductive in that something is left unsaid, something important in the meaning of the message.

SUMMARY

The process of human reason is complex. At no point can we be 100 percent certain of our evidence and our reasoning: Examples can be poorly chosen, metaphors can mislead, and deductions can lead to erroneous premises and conclusions. But reasoning is such a complex act that unless some sloppiness were allowed in the process, we wouldn't get anything done.

We use examples, definitions, statistics, and stories as illustration of and testimony to experience. We make comparisons and speak metaphorically. We engage in the process of induction when we add up our experiences, summarize our comparisons, and reach a general premise. We then use our premises to deduce our way to new propositions and conclusions.

PART TWO

TELEVISION CONTENT REVIEW

At one time just being on television would make you a star. But over thirty years of commercial television, plus increased access to television, have produced a number of outstanding models for television success. Such models, along with more sophisticated audiences, economic factors, and video availability, necessitate more reasoned uses of television. Television, while retaining its entertainment dimension, is increasingly a forum for evidenced and reasoned communication.

Illustration and testimony are two common forms of evidence in television messages. Common reasoning processes include comparison, induction, and deduction.

If you are doing an interview, illustration and testimony will substantiate your claims and enhance your credibility as a television speaker. If you are arguing company policy in a video conference, your ability to reason may well determine the success or failure of your presentation. In short, if you have a point to make, be your objective persuasion or information, then evidence and reason are particularly important in your television presentation.

RESOURCES

Notes

1. Gary Paul Gates, *Air Time: The Inside Story of CBS News* (New York: Berkeley Books, 1978), p. 64.
2. See Howard Rosenberg, "Afghanistan Coverage 'Alarming, Funny,' " *Las Vegas Review Journal,* 10 April 1980, p. 6F.
3. Donald K. Smith, *Man Speaking* (New York: Dodd, Mead, 1969), p. 130.
4. Aristotle, *Rhetoric,* Rhys Roberts, trans., (New York: Random House, 1954), p. 187.
5. Candiss Ann Baksa, *The Enthymeme in Television Advertising: A Logical Framework for Audience Participation,* master's thesis at the University of Nevada, Las Vegas, 1977.

Recommended Readings

KAHANE, HOWARD. *Logic and Contemporary Rhetoric: The Use of Reason in Everyday Life.* 4th ed. Belmont, Calif.: Wadsworth, 1984.

McCROSKEY, JAMES C. *An Introduction to Rhetorical Communication.* Englewood Cliffs, N.J.: Prentice-Hall, 1982.

NEWMAN, ROBERT P. and DALE R. *Evidence.* Boston: Houghton Mifflin, 1969.

TOULMIN, STEPHEN; RICHARD RIEKE; and ALLAN JANIK. *An Introduction to Reasoning.* New York: Macmillan, 1979.

PART TWO

TELEVISION CONTENT

KEY: 0 = Item does not apply
1 = Extremely well done
2 = Fairly well done
3 = Moderately well done
4 = Poorly done; needs improvement

CHAPTER 3. Evidence

	0	1	2	3	4
A. Use of illustrations (in general)	0	1	2	3	4
1. Use of definitions	0	1	2	3	4
2. Use of examples	0	1	2	3	4
3. Use of statistics	0	1	2	3	4
4. Use of stories	0	1	2	3	4
B. Use of testimony (in general)	0	1	2	3	4
1. Use of personal testimony	0	1	2	3	4
2. Use of impersonal testimony	0	1	2	3	4

CHAPTER 4. Reason

	0	1	2	3	4
A. Use of sound reasoning (in general)	0	1	2	3	4
1. Use of comparison	0	1	2	3	4
2. Use of induction	0	1	2	3	4
3. Use of deduction	0	1	2	3	4

PART THREE

STRUCTURING TELEVISION MESSAGES

It is the capacity for organizing information into large and complex images which is the chief glory of our species. . . .

Kenneth E. Boulding
The Image

The term *network* reflects the existence of organization in television communications. The word calls attention to interconnected facilities, channels, people, and ideas. The notion of interconnectedness is analogous to what faces television speakers. While they do not need to be interested or involved in the organization of television hardware, they must be concerned with the organization of their ideas and content.

The purpose of Part Three is to discuss general and particular forms of organization available to television speakers, and, specifically, to demonstrate how the beginning, middle, and end of a presentation constitute a general organizational pattern in television communication. Once we have discussed what we mean by general organizational pattern, we will then discuss a variety of specific organizational options possible in any given presentation.

Effective organization facilitates memory, retrieval, and delivery. Having your material organized not only makes it easier for you to explain the material to the other people involved in producing the videotape, but also for you to remember what you are doing and saying. Organization is an important aspect of television communication.

PART
THREE

5. THE GENERAL PATTERN OF ORGANIZATION

Two thousand years ago, in examining human discourse, Socrates suggested that it had a life of its own, had "a body of its own and a head and feet."[1] We tend, as Socrates suggested, to look for beginnings, middles, and ends. Traditionally, the major divisions of communication have been referred to as the introduction, the body, and the conclusion.

Introductions, bodies, conclusions are clearly present in contemporary television speaking. In *The Tonight Show,* for example, Johnny Carson is introduced and, in turn, offers an introductory monologue; his program then moves to a body that is composed of interviews by Carson of several guests (a form of interaction we discuss more specifically in Part Six); then a wrap-up ends the program.

At first glance, the basic ingredients of organization seem simple. However, closer examination reveals that introductions, bodies, and conclusions are composed of numerous elements. Introductions, among other things, seize attention, establish relationships, reveal purpose, and offer a preview of ensuing material. Bodies involve the content mentioned in the previous chapter and the astute use of transitions. Conclusions entail reiteration and the attempt to leave an afterimage. Introductions, bodies, and conclusions are central components in the arrangement of a television message.

THE INTRODUCTION

Introductions are commonly associated with (1) the gaining of attention; (2) the establishment of relationships between speaker, audience, and subject; (3) statements of purpose; and (4) statements of method.

Gaining Attention

Getting the contemporary audience to pay attention is not an easy accomplishment. Consider all that you have seen on television and then think about what it takes for your attention to be drawn and held by a television event.

Novel, deep, and startling statements have been considered good openers, as have humor, unusual sounds, and extravagant visuals. Let us look at a few of these devices and see how they might help you gain attention:

Novel:	Today when I talk about dog training, I'll take the position that there are no bad dogs, only bad dog owners. *We* need training—not the dogs. Let me explain.
Deep:	Last month in our city, 51 percent of all the black males were unemployed. They were out of work and on the streets. If we don't begin to focus on this problem, these young people are going to get angry, frustrated, and restless . . . and with good cause!
Humorous:	Today I'd like to talk to you about your budget. You know what a budget is. It is a method of worrying about your money *before* it is spent—not afterwards.
Startling:	Predictions are that robots, not people, will soon be working at 92 percent of most factory jobs. What about the individuals that they will replace?

Establishing Relationships

Once you've gained the attention of your viewers, you then face the task of establishing a relationship with them, one based on your characteristics, their characteristics, and the subject of your presentation. In Part One we talked about the human variables of television communication. In the introduction of your television presentation you should draw heavily upon those variables.

In establishing a relationship with your audience, you must begin by asking yourself what you believe the audience will think of you. Will they welcome your message? Will they be friendly? Hostile? Will they perceive you as credible? The answers will help you determine how to maintain rapport with your viewers—whether you should try to seem serious or jovial, pensive or relaxed. This analysis should even tell you whether you should walk, stand, or sit. If you reflect for a moment, you will see how your posture, at least in the early stages of the program, will influence your relationship with the audience.

Alistair Cooke, for example, often introduces himself seated in an armchair, looking directly at the audience, seeming comfortable and at home. Cooke develops an interpersonal relationship with his audience, one that exudes personal warmth. Not all television situations warrant an interpersonal approach; however, some sense of relationship is apparent in every television presentation. Introductions generally establish the relationship.

Statement of Purpose

Why is the speaker speaking and the listener listening? In the broadest sense, the question is whether persuasion, information, or entertainment is the primary goal. As we have mentioned, the purpose of an address isn't always stated explicitly. You have to decide how clear you wish to be in your statements of motive. On most occasions you should be direct and straightforward, as in saying, "Today I would like to talk to you about the correct way to select vitamins."

General Preview

A preview of *Hill Street Blues* shows the highlights of the upcoming segment. An anchor person previews the highlights of the evening's news. Most television presentations involve some sense of preview.

The sample script in Part Four of this book illustrates clear, concise previewing. The speaker indicates what will be discussed first, second, and third. Such ordering lends clarity to a presentation and helps the speaker and the audience remember its major points.

Even though short, introductions can be complex; they must gain attention, establish relationships and purpose, and provide a preview.

Obviously, to produce a successful introduction, you need to have given considerable thought to the body of your address. No matter how witty or insightful your introduction may be, it is the body of the presentation that bears the weight of your message.

THE BODY

David K. Berlo has noted in *The Process of Communication* that content is like code in that it has both elements and structure: "If you try to present three pieces of information, you have to present them in some order. One has to come first, one last."[2] If you've prepared yourself for your presentation, you have marshalled your material. But before you present it, you must structure it. For any body of material, there may be an infinite number of arrangements. Like musical notes, communication content can be ordered in various ways, to suit the speaker, the situation, and the audience.

As we've already noted, the primary structuring of a television message is achieved by time limits. It's likely that not all of your material will fit in the time available, so you must make decisions: You must edit out the least significant data and arrange what remains in order of importance. You must decide which should come first and which should come last.

Ordering your content is essential for any type of television presentation. If you are a surgeon performing an operation on closed-circuit television and creating a videotape for other doctors and medical students, then the material of the presentation must clearly follow the order dictated by the operation. The order must be clear in order to perform the operation successfully, and the order must be clear if the operation is to be videotaped successfully.

Transitions

You must do more than arrange the order of your address, however. There is nothing more boring than fact piled on fact. To make your material palatable to an audience, you must devise transitions that will move it from point to point. (Transitions are discussed further in Chapter 13.)

Carl Sagan is a television speaker who uses transitions well. He doesn't just blurt out his material; he pieces it together like a mosaic artfully glued together by transitions. In one show, while talking about the development of a scientific principle, he situated himself in an outdoor café, a popular gathering place for the scientists under discussion. Then, as he verbally moved away from the particular point being discussed, he physically walked away from the café, down the road to a beach. The musical equivalent of Sagan's walk is called a *bridge*. The term aptly describes what a transition does in human address: It connects two points.

Internal summaries are a common form of transition. They allow your viewers to follow and understand your message even if they've just tuned in to your presentation. For example: "Having just looked at some of the false claims made by many vitamin manufacturers, let me now turn to a discussion of the types of vitamins that are most useful."

THE CONCLUSION

In Chapter 1 we talked about some of the differences between ordinary conversation and television communication, noting that the distractions inherent in television production are sometimes overwhelming. One of those distractions often occurs in the conclusion of a presentation.

In a normal conversation you can usually meander through your conclusion in whatever time you require. In television, you may be halfway through a point and suddenly find that you are being given the thirty-second sign. It takes five seconds for the meaning to hit you; you now have twenty-five seconds to wrap up your immediate conversation. What do you do?

Conclusions are basically reiterations. In reviewing your material, you have choices; your primary choice is one of degree. To what extent do you summarize your presentation? If you have the time, you can hark back to your introductory material, pointing out how your preview has been fulfilled, and you can re-emphasize the purpose of your presentation while reviewing its content. For example: "Today we looked at the importance of vitamins in your daily life. We talked about some false claims made by those who try to sell you vitamins and some standards that you should apply when purchasing vitamins."

But in situations where you're likely to be faced with the necessity for a quick conclusion, you would do well to have rehearsed various possibilities. What you are seeking might best be described as an **afterimage,** like the image that lingers on a television screen after the scene has changed or when the set is turned off. Alistair Cooke renders an afterimage to *Masterpiece Theater* by referring to one striking point about the production, then settling back in his chair as he offers his final words; we are left with this frozen image.

SUMMARY

Our perception of events as continuous makes pinpointing exact beginnings, middles, and ends a difficult task. But just as we think of human life and geologic formations in terms of youth, middle, and old age, so we assimilate and communicate events in terms of beginnings, middles, and ends.

What we've outlined thus far is a pattern of organization, one that can be applied to almost any act of communication. This general scheme of beginnings, middles, and ends is just that, a general scheme—within it you can divide material further, by means of specific organizational forms, which we discuss in the following chapter.

6. SPECIFIC FORMS OF ORGANIZATION

Long before you picked up this book you were preparing to be on television. This preparation took the form of watching and judging others communicating on television. Having a sense of general organization is only half your task; how you organize the details that make up the body of your presentation is the other half. Six specific forms of organization are particularly apparent in television: sequential, question–answer, tradition, theme, problem–solution, and motivation. You may not wish to use all of them in your presentation; however, knowing the various forms enhances your ability to make the most of your television opportunities.

SEQUENTIAL ORGANIZATION

In organizing your material sequentially, you follow one of two patterns: space or time.

Space

Spatial organization is a means of orienting the listener to the path of the speaker. By establishing points of reference, by creating a general overall picture of an event, you familiarize the audience with the territory being covered.

The movie *It's a Mad, Mad, Mad, Mad World* epitomizes organization based on space. The plot revolves around a treasure hunt. People in different places, all with the same map, begin moving through space toward a specific point. Such movement is common in television presentations. For example, in the old television series *Route 66,* the plot was based on two young men moving from point to point on a highway. The evening news is often based on the same organizational principle: A map is shown and arrows are drawn to demonstrate movement in a war, a disease, a weather front. The speaker moves the audience through a sequence that is easy to follow.

In an interview you can hinge your presentation on spatial reference. You can explain how you got from a certain beginning point to your present situation at the time of the interview. Guests on talk shows often talk about their experiences in strange environments; such stories are almost always of interest to general audiences. In a televised job interview you could organize a part of your presentation around where you have lived or worked.

By organizing your message around spaces that you know and understand, you give yourself a clue to remembering the sequence of what you have to say. The spatial dimension of your material gives your audience a memory aid as well. It may also help them to relate to your point. Insofar as the audience has any familiarity with the space you define, they can identify with you and your message.

Time

Human mortality makes time an obsession. We divide our lifetimes into years, months, weeks, days, hours, minutes, and seconds. As we continue to point out, time is always a constraint in television communication. It's also a basis for sequencing a television message.

Time, like space, has been a common basis of sequential organization in television. Each episode of *Star Trek,* for example, began with date and time. The evening news usually begins the same way. And each episode of the news tends to rely on time as the basic organizational principle.

If your presentation will be aired through commercial outlets, you should organize your address to fit the time blocks allowed. If there is a sequence of commercials every five minutes, arrange your material to accommodate these breaks.

Like space, time is a means of familiarizing your audience with your point. Establishing a temporal framework for your message also helps you and your audience remember your material, as well as allowing them to place themselves within the time context and relate more personally to what you are saying.

Just as a job interview might be organized on the basis of places worked, so might it be organized according to time spent in different job situations and training. As a talk show guest, you can make time the basic organizational principle of your presentation. Establishing a time sequence in your material enhances its reality and lends it precision.

QUESTION–ANSWER FORMAT

As we'll note in Part Six, interviewing is one of the most common of television experiences. News programs, talk shows, game shows all rely on the Q&A format. As with sequential organization, organization based on questions and answers may be a dominant arrangement or may be one of several overlaid patterns.

In everyday dialogue, question–answer sessions can be pointless and meandering. In television, given the constraints of time and the expectation that a program go somewhere and have a purpose, some effort should be made to ensure that the conversation has a direction, that the questions and answers are both interesting and informative.

If you are the interviewer, you have a series of questions prepared, and they form a natural basis of organization. For example, if you were conducting an employment interview via a teleconference system, you might start with general questions ("How are you today?") and then move to more specific questions ("Why are you leaving your current position?"). This movement from general to specific is an effective organizational pattern. If you are the interviewee on a talk or news show, and if it is at all possible, you would do well to have the list of questions before airtime, so that you will be on the same organizational track as the questioner.

The question–answer format can be used with different motives, two of which are particularly important to television speakers: inquiry and proving a presupposed point.

In inquiry, the questioner is genuinely seeking an answer about something that is unknown ("Tell us, why did your company move its factory from our city?"). In such a case the interviewee may become an active participant in the ensuing discussion and produce questions and answers not considered by the interviewer. In a question–answer session that is approached in the spirit of inquiry, knowledge is the goal.

Some question–answer sessions are not so much intended to inform as they are to prove a point. For example, when Mike Wallace bears down on an interviewee, his questions are as often as not determined by a position he holds. Indeed, some critics feel that *60 Minutes*'s advocacy stance often mars its informative effect. Lawsuits and complaints against the program have indicated that asking loaded questions and leading witnesses can distort information.

If you are being interviewed, facing unfair questions, and can see that the question–answer format is more advocacy-oriented than information-oriented, you have decisions to make. You can challenge the interviewer and advance your own position ("I think that your question fails to look at the problem. What really happened was . . ."), or ask your own leading questions and produce your own answers ("Imagine what you would do if you were in my place. Let me take a minute and suggest what you would do.").

In preparing for question–answer presentations, it is often helpful to have your colleagues run you through a series of trials.

TRADITIONAL PATTERNS

In the thirty years that television has been popular, thousands of programs have come and gone as different styles and subjects have been tried and failed. Those programs that have succeeded have established program-types based on specific organizational patterns.

For example, individual soap operas have been premiered and canceled, but the pattern remains. Soaps operas tend to begin with a flashback so that new viewers can get some idea of what's transpired in the story and fans can have their memories refreshed. The body of a soap opera is generally organized around a certain number of characters, each receiving concentrated attention at different times throughout the show. The conclusion is usually the beginning of a new episode—which serves to leave the audience hanging.

News programs are another example of how organization can become standardized. We are introduced to an anchor who briefly reviews or highlights the day's events, then comes a commercial, followed by specific stories that are handled by reporters and crews around the world and punctuated by commercials. Sports, weather, and human-interest stories conclude the news, and it fades into another block of commercials.

Any program-type that has been around for any length of time has been through considerable experimentation, and from that testing have emerged preferred methods of organization. If what you're preparing for television bears any resemblance to a common program-type, examine those programs similar to yours. A common organizational pattern for the program-type may emerge and may suggest a form of organization suitable to your presentation. For example, if you are asked by your firm to put a series of training programs on tape so that new employees can view them, look at the structure of educational programs that have been successful. Go to your local college or university and examine their video materials. Notice if they use a traditional organizational scheme: beginning by gaining attention, attempting to motivate the viewer, previewing main points, offering their material in an interesting and clear manner, and concluding with a summary.

Keep in mind that using a tested and successful scheme of organization is no guarantee that your presentation will be a smash. As we've noted, many programs have failed, even though they may have followed a formula that had worked in the past. Even the best of organizational patterns can become dull and outdated.

Experimentation is often the key to a successful presentation. If you have control over your material, try organizing your presentation in various ways. If you have the equipment and resources to videotape your presentation using several types of organization, reviewing the reruns with friends and a carefully selected audience should tell you which is the best.

ORGANIZATION BY THEME

In music, a theme is a melody that recurs and comes to characterize the song. Conversation, like song, has thematic organization. Many television productions are built around a basic theme, a basic idea that is stated several times throughout.

Themes are particularly apparent in commercials. For example, in the Toyota series, the car is described and the viewer is told that there is a feeling with Toyota that is unique; the musical and conceptual theme becomes "Oh, what a feeling!"

In thematic organization, a body of material is punctuated by a recurring refrain. If you are being interviewed and there is some particular point that you wish to make, you can periodically return to it: "Throughout our discussion I have been trying to stress the idea that our department is doing everything it can to encourage our female students to take part in sports. It is our contention that the opportunity for fitness should not be decided by gender."

Thematic organization can also be found in educational television presentations. One of the authors once taught a fifteen-week televised class on communication. Each program was organized around the theme "Communication is a decision-making process." So while each show treated a different decision, the main theme was a common thread woven into all the programs.

In *Sesame Street,* numbers, colors, and the subjects of basic education are thematically developed. In *The Ascent of Man,* an educational program for adults, the basic theme was that there was progress in human affairs through science; each episode was organized around that theme.

Themes are also part of entertainment presentations. Themes of good and evil, rich and poor, smart and stupid are common in soap operas and prime-time television. Themes have always been essential to literature, and are as apparent in television as they have been in print.

Thematic organization may intermingle with other forms of organization and may be dominant or subordinate to them. Like all forms of organization, arrangement through theme helps you and your listener remember the point.

PROBLEM–SOLUTION ARRANGEMENTS

Several years ago, on the East Coast, a television system called "the new rural society" was established for various professional communications. The system enabled doctors, lawyers, teachers, politicians, and others to bridge the gap between rural and urban populations. For example, a doctor in a rural area with a two-way video hookup and a phone connection to the medical instruments in an urban clinic could practice medicine even though considerably removed from the patient. The basic organization for such communication is problem–solution.

Problem–solution organization is as apparent in network productions as in experimental programs. Most private eye melodramas begin with a crime that requires solution; most soap operas focus on a series of problems that beg for solution; talk shows often feature guests who have developed solutions for particular problems. Because problems are so much a part of our existence, they provide a handy basis for the organization of communication.

Two essential ingredients lead to problem–solution arrangements: suspense and exigency. **Suspense** is the stuff of most detective stories. Suspense is also the basic material of genuine inquiry—a search automatically creates suspense. If your television presentation has any element of suspense, then you should consider a problem–solution arrangement of your material.

Exigency is a situation of need, a situation that demands attention and response. *60 Minutes* has its general human interest stories, but its central organizing principle has been problems that require solution. If you are dealing with exigencies that you and your audience share, then a problem–solution arrangement seems appropriate.

Whether you are considering a television job interview, a tele-conference, or a talk show, a problem–solution arrangement of your materials may suit your organizational needs. Like the other forms of organization mentioned in this chapter, the problem/solution arrangement is simply one more option available to the television speaker.

ORGANIZATION BY MOTIVE

In Chapter 2 we said that speakers normally have specific reasons for appearing on television—to persuade, inform, or entertain. The intent of a speaker can suggest specific organizational forms.

Persuasion

Persuasion, one of the most studied of human motives, suggests a particular form of organization. Alan Monroe has observed persuasion to have five steps:

1. An attention step

2. A problem/need step that clarifies a problem

3. A satisfaction step that explains a solution to the problem

4. A visualization step that envisions how the world will look if the satisfaction step is taken

5. An action step in which the speaker makes specific recommendations for the audience.[3]

Monroe's motivated sequence is a common one in television address. There is not a commercial made, political or mercantile, that fails to strive first to seize the viewers' concentrated attention. Next it establishes some need (perhaps for personal hygiene, perhaps for well-being, perhaps for health) and some means of satisfying it (a soap, a car, a medicine). Once the solution has been suggested, there is some portrayal of a satisfied customer. And finally, there is the specific advice to "get right down to your local dealer."

Information

The desire to inform, like the desire to persuade, can lead to specific methods of organization. An informative presentation can be organized according to the method of reasoning used, for example, induction or deduction. *Sesame Street* gives example after example of how two apples, two oranges, and two of anything share the concept of 2; the process is clearly inductive.

Deductive reasoning was a major presence in *Cosmos,* an adult-oriented educational program. Host Carl Sagan would present a certain number of examples that led to a certain conclusion. He would then point out that if the conclusion were true, other facts might be determined. If, for example, Einstein's theory of relativity were true, then other guesses about the universe could be made.

Entertainment

If your purpose is to entertain your audience, your material may be amenable to the common organizational methods of plot and skit.

Plots are storylines. In every plot, there are pieces left out, pieces filled in by the actors, actresses, directors, producers, and every other member of the video team. The plot organizes the whole into a cohesive unit.

A **skit** is a story within a story. *Saturday Night Live* and *Laugh-In* are examples of entertaining television organized around a body of skits. Individual performers, as well as groups of performers, use skits as the organizational skeleton of their work.

Regardless of the organizational scheme you select, try to adhere to the following recommendations.

1. *Know your material.* By being familiar with your facts, figures, testimony, illustrations, and the like, you can better decide how to organize your presentation.

2. *Observe and compare.* There are probably examples of television productions similar to what you wish to do. How is their material organized? How do they begin? What makes up the bulk of their presentation? How do they conclude?

   When we suggest observation, we mean more than observation of others. Review your own material closely. Home videotaping units can help refine your presentation (we discuss this further in Part Four). Even with the most rudimentary equipment, you can capture and make judgments about the organization of your work.

3. *Simplify.* Simplicity is important in television presentations. As we pointed out earlier, time is generally limited in television

communications. You can't cover everything in a one-shot deal. Also keep in mind that three major points are easier to remember than six. As audiences become increasingly sophisticated, as new channels emerge, as specialized audiences are focused on, television does gain organizational complexity. But the general rule remains: Strive for simplicity, particularly if you're undertaking your first exposure to the camera.

4. *Experiment*. The general outline of organization and the seven particular forms of organization that we discussed in this section are not ironclad fixtures of all human communication. There are streams of consciousness, there are trains of thought that do not lend themselves to organizational control—there is poetry.

Your material, your life experiences, the particular situation that brings you to use television, and thousands of other variables may lead you to an untested organizational form. The only way to determine whether the new form will work is to try it out.

In recommending experimentation, we do not mean to imply that you should experiment on the air. Do it before you air your presentation so that you telecast the form that best presents you and your material. The sources listed at the end of this part may further assist you in organizing your television content.

Sequence, inquiry, tradition, theme, problems, and motives—each can be the basis of how we organize our communications. There are, no doubt, myriad other bases of organization. Only you can decide which is best for you.

PART
THREE

STRUCTURING TELEVISION MESSAGES

REVIEW

As a business, television requires organization in its office, technical, personnel, and transmission operations. As a form of communication, it is generally a tightly scheduled, well-organized medium. If you are a part of a television presentation, you are a part of an organized effort, and you will be expected to have your part of the presentation well organized.

Organization in television communication involves the organization of time. It is important to know the total amount of time you have and the breaks that may occur in your presentation. Even more important, the material that you bring to a presentation must be organized. Most presentations have beginnings, middles, and ends. Beyond the general organizational formats offered in this section, there are a multitude of options.

Organization is important to television speakers in several ways. Having your material organized makes it easier (1) for you to explain the material to the people involved in producing the videotape; (2) for you to remember what you are doing; (3) for your audience to follow and understand your reasoning.

RESOURCES

Notes

1. Plato, "Phaedrus," *The Dialogues of Plato,* B. Jowett, trans. (London: Oxford University Press, 1968), p. 173.
2. David K. Berlo, *The Process of Communication* (New York: Holt, Rinehart and Winston, 1960), p. 59.
3. Alan Monroe, *Principles and Types of Speech,* Third Edition (Chicago: Scott, Foresman, 1975), p. 308.

Recommended Readings

BETTINGHAUS, ERWIN P. *Message Preparation: The Nature of Proof.* New York: Bobbs-Merrill, 1966.

FETZER, RONALD C., and ROBERT A. VOGEL. *Designing Messages.* Chicago: Science Research Associates, 1982.

MILLS, GLEN E. *Message Preparation: Analysis and Structure.* New York: Bobbs-Merrill, 1966.

SAMOVAR, LARRY A., and JACK MILLS. *Oral Communication: Message and Response.* Dubuque, Iowa: William C. Brown, 1983.

PART THREE

STRUCTURING TELEVISION MESSAGES

KEY: 0 = Item does not apply
       1 = Extremely well done
       2 = Fairly well done
       3 = Moderately well done
       4 = Poorly done; needs improvement

CHAPTER 5. The General Pattern of Organization

A. The Introduction (in general)	0	1	2	3	4
1. Gaining attention	0	1	2	3	4
2. Establishing relationships	0	1	2	3	4
3. Statement of purpose	0	1	2	3	4
4. General preview	0	1	2	3	4
B. The Body (in general)	0	1	2	3	4
1. Organization of the presentation	0	1	2	3	4
2. Transitions	0	1	2	3	4
C. The Conclusion (in general)	0	1	2	3	4
1. Reviewed material	0	1	2	3	4
2. Re-emphasized purpose	0	1	2	3	4

CHAPTER 6. Specific Forms of Organization

A. Use of specific organizational forms (in general)	0	1	2	3	4
1. Use of sequential forms	0	1	2	3	4
2. Use of question–answer forms	0	1	2	3	4
3. Use of traditional forms	0	1	2	3	4
4. Use of theme forms	0	1	2	3	4
5. Use of problem–solution forms	0	1	2	3	4
6. Use of motivational forms	0	1	2	3	4

PART FOUR

THE TELEVISION STUDIO

studio   *The workroom of a sculptor or painter*

OED

Throughout this book we have alluded to the fact that high-quality television, in both format and content, is a collaborative effort. In Chapter 7 we will thoroughly discuss studio staff so that you might better understand how their duties affect your performance. In addition, we will examine the language and procedures of the studio. In order for everyone involved in the formulation of television messages to understand one another, a specialized language has been developed, in verbal, gesticulative, and print forms. It is continually added to as more and more people and equipment become involved in the use of television.

Part of being successful on television is knowing what is expected of you: what you should do next, where you should sit (or stand), and where you should look (and when). These and other mysteries of proper studio procedure are usually solved during a rehearsal when all involved have an opportunity to polish their particular part of the presentation. Rehearsals will also be discussed in Chapter 7.

The language of television demands special equipment. For people focused on their own occupations, preoccupations, and personal dialogue, the equipment of television is bothersome. As bothersome as it may be, however, it is a necessity. In Chapters 8 and 9 we will talk about the primary and secondary tools of television production: cameras, microphones, recorders, switchers, character generators, editors, and visuals.

The workings of the studio are complex, but, as we note in the next three chapters, that complexity eases with practice. First-rate television communication requires the acceptance of some complexity, as well as an awareness and appreciation of the staff, tools, and methods of the television studio.

PART
FOUR

7. PERSONNEL, PARLANCE, AND PROCEDURES

Although there are many different types of studios, they share some common characteristics. Most professional studios are made up of two interconnected rooms that house the equipment and personnel needed to put the program on the air (or on tape). The first room, the **set** or **floor,** has cameras, lights, microphones, yards of cable, props, scenery, and the people who operate the hardware (this is also the room where you face the camera).

The second room, called the **control room,** is where yet another group of colleagues perform their jobs. The control room looks like a scene from a space shuttle—a welter of consoles and controls, monitor sets, switches, dials, and meters. Unless you're intending to become a television engineer, you may never fully understand the set and control-room equipment. Yet you should be familiar with the basics of production so that you can communicate with studio personnel.

We should point out that, while we repeatedly use the word *studio* to describe the place of the production, television programs are often produced on location. While there are a few minor adjustments you might have to make to your delivery for performances on location (we

Figure 7.1 The set (or floor).

The camera operator is preparing for a rehearsal about to begin. Note that there are two cameras; in rehearsal, they will be positioned at different locations so that it will be possible to cut between close-ups of the interviewer and the guest.

will discuss these in Chapters 10 and 11), the bulk of the alterations are the responsibility of the technical staff, not the speaker.

STUDIO PERSONNEL

When you first walk into the studio of a major network or an established television system, you can't help being impressed, if not overwhelmed, by what seem to be countless people moving in countless directions. However, once you've spent even a small amount of time in the studio, you'll begin to recognize who these people are and what they are

Figure 7.2
**The control room equipment can appear intimidating
to a novice.**

doing. Our experience indicates that in most productions you can expect
to find the following people in the studio: producers, directors, floor
managers, floor crews, technical crews, and production assistants.

For some small-scale programs, the "production crew" may be made
up of one or two people—and one of them might be you! We have been
involved in productions where a single individual served as producer, director, audio engineer, switcher, and writer. Productions done on location
(away from the studio) and those using inexpensive hand-held units usually fall into this category.

Producer

The producer's job is not an easy one. When you meet this person in the
studio, you can be sure that he or she will be busy. You are just one of a
host of variables the producer must juggle. The vast scope of the producer's assignment is clearly noted by Alan Wurtzel in his book, *Television Production:*

Figure 7.3

**"On location" refers to anywhere outside the television
studio. Here a program is being taped in the subject's
workplace.**

*Television's answer to the Renaissance man is the television pro-
ducer. This is because a producer has to know a little about a lot.
Since the producer is responsible for every element in a show, he or
she must be sufficiently knowledgeable in all areas of production.* [1]

The producer must not only be aware of all phases of production,
from inception to evaluation, but must be responsible for a number of
crucial decisions as well. Among other things, the producer may have
proposed the program, analyzed its potential audience, decided on its
budget, raised the necessary funds, decided on possible production methods, dealt with the production staff as well as possible investors, scheduled facilities and equipment, coordinated talent, and made arrangements for the program to be evaluated after it has been aired. As
you can see, the producer must be able to manage ideas, people, and
activities.

In large, expensive, and complex productions some of the producer's
chores are handled by other people. An executive producer will oversee

the production, while other people with titles such as assistant or associate producer will deal with certain specific areas of programming: talent, script, budget, etc. In the case of most noncommercial enterprises, one person often serves as both producer and director.

Director

While the producer is concerned with issues in and out of the studio, the director's main concern is the actual production. He or she is the boss, in charge of directing the presentation and the technical staff. In general terms, it is the director who will determine the creative form the program will take. By combining the video with the audio, the director decides what images the viewers will receive.

The director's numerous responsibilities are carried out during all phases of the production. Before the program is actually broadcast, the director must review and evaluate the script, decide on blocking, coordinate and evaluate the rehearsal, time the program, and supervise everyone on the set and in the control room (this means both on-camera and off-camera personnel). What is particularly challenging about the director's role *during* the production is that he or she must communicate with the staff while the program is "on." This is accomplished through a rather elaborate electronic system of monitors and headsets and through hand signals used by the floor manager.

The multidimensional aspect of directing is well illustrated by Herbert Zettl in the following list of activities that the director must undertake while shooting a simple, two-camera show. (A glossary of technical terms on pp. 89–92 will define any terms you don't understand.)

> *(1) Talk and listen to studio engineers and production crew: camera operators, microphone boom operator, floor manager, floorpersons; (2) converse with the people in the control room, telecine, and VTR room: T.D., audio engineer, light board operator, telecine operator, videotape operator, character generator operator, and master control engineers; (3) watch at least six monitors all the time: two camera preview, telecine, VTR, general preview, and line; (4) watch the time: the control-room clock for the schedule (or log) times, and the stopwatch for the running times of the individual show segments and inserts; (5) listen to the program audio . . . , and (6) follow the script.[2]*

From this description you can see that the director is a busy and probably harried person who would be happy to have your cooperation. Try to establish rapport at the first meeting by indicating that you understand the complexity of his or her assignment.

Figure 7.4

The director checks out a camera angle before
rehearsal begins. Photography by Scott Highton.
Courtesy of Over Easy/KQED.

Floor Manager

The floor manager, often referred to as the stage manager, is one of the central characters in the production staff. He or she is in charge of the set or remote location while the director is in the control room or remote truck.

The floor manager serves as the link between the director and the people on the set (this means the performers as well as the production crew). In many instances you will have more face-to-face contact with the floor managers than with directors. Because they are directly in front of you, they will try to put you at ease during rehearsal and production, by activities ranging from offering you water to giving you advice on how to improve your performance. They are also the ones who will explain studio procedure and protocol. If something goes wrong during rehearsal, the floor manager will explain what has happened and how long it will take to get back on schedule. The floor manager also gives you cues, signals, and other advice during the time you are in the studio.

As we noted, the floor manager is in charge of the members of the crew that are on the set. Working through the director, he or she will assist in the placement and movement of props, performers, graphics, and the like—even direct the switching of lights, microphones, and cameras. In small productions, the floor manager may do the actual moving of this equipment.

Not only do floor managers work with you and the crew during the performance but—when labor union constraints don't apply—they may have a number of important responsibilities before the other members of the crew arrive. They are involved in all preproduction conferences, help set up the lights, props, cameras, graphics, cables, and also coordinate the floor positions that everyone will take once the rehearsal begins. In short, the floor manager has the responsibility to make sure that everything runs smoothly on the set.

Floor Crew

We use the term *floor crew* to refer to all those people who perform their duties on the main studio floor rather than in the control room. As you would suspect, the number of people needed on the floor, and their specific tasks, is contingent on several factors: budget, purpose of the show, potential audience, location, complexity of the program, and available personnel and equipment. Nonetheless, we can look at some of the personnel you may meet on the set of some studios.

CAMERA OPERATORS   Whether there are two or eight of them, the duty of the camera operators is basically the same: to operate the camera smoothly so that the visual element of the broadcast is aesthetically pleasing. Most camera operators have a good visual sense and understand the importance of form and composition. A camera, as we will discuss later in more detail, is capable of a multiplicity of different movements and shots. And while the director often tells the camera operator how to

Figure 7.5

The camera operators are always in contact with the director. Note how the use of imaginative lighting augments a very simple set.

arrive at those positions and angles, it is the operator who actually sets up the shot and introduces his or her creativity into the production.

BOOM OPERATOR   The audio portion of the production is the responsibility of the microphone boom operator. This person sees to it that the overhead microphone is out of camera range yet close enough to pick up the audio segments of the program. If a lavaliere, hand-held, or stand microphone is used, the audio person will usually take on another assignment once the microphones have been properly situated and tested.

LIGHT BOARD OPERATOR   Without lighting, either natural or artificial, there is no video. Most productions also have someone who is responsible for lighting. This person must make sure that the set and the performers can be seen. In smaller productions the person in charge of lighting might have some additional jobs to perform, such as helping arrange furniture, assisting with audio checks, and even applying some make-up to the performers.

Technical Crew

The people who carry out the bulk of their assignments in the control room have a variety of jobs, and you should become familiar with some of them.

TECHNICAL DIRECTOR   The technical director (often called the **switcher**) sits next to the program director, in front of the production console, a large bank of buttons, knobs, and controls, and operates the **switcher.** This device allows the technical director, on the advice of the program director, to place any one of a number of video sources on the air. Specifically, the switcher, controlled by the technical director, performs three basic functions: (1) selecting the appropriate video input from one of several monitors in the control room; (2) effecting a transition from one video source to another (by dissolving and cutting); and (3) creating special effects by switching from one source to another. (We will discuss the switcher in greater detail in Chapter 9.)

At some smaller studios there is no technical director; the program director must operate the switcher. Looking at the monitors in the control room, the program director selects the shots, tapes, or graphics.

AUDIO ENGINEER   Most control rooms will have an audio engineer (sometimes called the **audio technician**) who is also seated in front of the main production console. Audio engineers are in charge of all sound operations. This, of course, involves much more than turning microphones on and off. While they do adjust volume levels, they also make aesthetic judgments, listen for and screen out extraneous noises, integrate audio messages (music, off-camera voices, etc.), and help regulate the tone and quality of the performer's voice. In smaller productions, these engineers are also in charge of the tape recorders, record turntables, and other audio equipment.

Production Assistants

If you are part of an expensive and elaborate program, you may find that the studio floor and the control room resemble a major downtown intersection. Many studios employ, in addition to the people we have already discussed, some of the following personnel:

Assistant directors to help the program director in specific areas

Music directors to supervise all musical aspects of the production

Scenic designers to help decide on and arrange the sets

Wardrobe experts to help dress the performers

Makeup artists to select and apply the makeup

Graphics experts to help design and coordinate any visuals that might be needed in the production of titles, still photographs, drawings, and the like

Videotape engineers to oversee the use of the videotape equipment

Property directors to arrange and often to move the scenery and props

Dolly pushers to move the camera dolly from place to place so that the camera person can concentrate on securing the best shot

Writers to supervise and edit their work

Secretaries to take notes

Facilities directors to oversee and coordinate all of the operations on the set

The studio is filled with a great many people who have specific tasks to perform. So it is important to remember that while they are there to help you accomplish your communication purpose, they also have their own problems to worry about. If you are sympathetic, show concern and interest, and understand their duties, they will work productively with you.

PARLANCE

It is not enough simply to understand the jobs of the people you will encounter in the studio; you must also be able to communicate with them. What do you do when the floor manager says to you, "Disregard the ann. line and the boom—we've decided to do the action without the audio on this run"? What is your reaction when someone in front of you starts making circles in the air with his finger while you are talking? Knowing the language of the studio—learning the specialized vocabulary and gestures—will keep you from being confused.

Vocabulary

Every profession adopts jargon—certain words and phrases to describe, define, and explain the objects and behaviors in their environment. Television is no exception. A rather extensive list of words and gestures is used before, during, and after the production. Following are a few of the more important words and gestures that you should become familiar with as part of your training program. Learning this language will help you overcome studio stupefaction—you will be able to talk to the people on the set and understand what they are saying when they talk to you. This in turn will enable you to relax and concentrate on accomplishing your purpose.

Ad lib   (n) An action or speech that has no written script; (v) to perform such an action or make such a speech.

Action   A verbal cue given by the director to indicate the performance (production) should begin.

Ann.   In a script, indicates announcer's part either on or off camera.

Arcing   A combination trucking, panning, and dollying movement, in which the camera is moved in an arc around a subject while the lens is always pointed toward the same subject.

Audio   The sound portion of a program.

Blackout   Having the camera fade to total black. Often a transition from one scene to another.

Blocking   The plotting of action for the equipment and performers by the director during rehearsals.

Boom   Cranelike device suspending microphone or cameras.

Buses   The rows of buttons representing various video sources on the switcher.

Busy   (adj) Of background—so elaborate and/or detailed that it often distorts the image being projected, producing flickers and jiggling on the screen.

Character generator   A computerized typewriter that inserts lettering into the picture.

Closed circuit   Not transmitted. A program fed to limited and selected points.

Control room   Area where director, technical director, audio engineer, and the like work during the program.

Crawl   A moving roll of credits or other messages on the screen.

Cue   A start or stop signal for actors, sound, and/or music. Can be verbal or nonverbal.

Cue cards   *See* **idiot cards.**

Cutaway   A camera shot diverted from the main action of the performer.

Dissolve   (n) An overlapping of shots. The image of the first shot mingles with the shot coming in.

Dolly in (dolly out)   To move the camera in toward (or away from) the performer or action.

Dry run   The initial rehearsal without cameras, in or outside the studio.

Fade in (fade out)   To have the camera come in (or out) of the scene gradually.

Fader bars   Small levers on the switcher that control the amount of video signal flowing to a particular bus.

Film chain (telecine)   An island of equipment—film projectors, a slide projector, a multiplexer, etc.

From the top   Start again from the beginning.

Graphics   Two-dimensional visuals—cards, flat pictures, printed signs.

Headset   An earphone and mouthpiece that connects production personnel to the intercom network.

Hold   To stop all movement and action.

Idiot cards   Large cards with lines of speech, dialogue, or cues written on them. Usually hand-held, easy to see, and off camera.

Kill   To cut and/or stop the action that is going on.

Level   Audio volume; "get a level" means to check the amount of volume.

Line monitor   Displays for the director all the possible scenes he or she can select; also shows final program picture that is to be recorded or transmitted.

Marks   Taped or painted lines on the studio floor indicating positions where the performers are to stand.

Monitor   A screen on which the control-room personnel can view the pictures being broadcast. There is often a monitor in the studio for the performers to glance at—but don't get caught gazing at yourself.

Multiplexer   An instrument that employs mirrors and prisms to reflect from different projectors into one camera.

Pan   (v) To move the camera horizontally while the pedestal remains stationary. (n) This kind of shot.

P. D.   Program director.

Pedestal   A mechanism on which a camera can be placed that allows it to be raised or lowered, usually by hydraulic means.

Playback   (n) A check on audio or videotape, usually immediately after recording.

Punch-up   (n) Shows the scene selected by the director—the one being broadcast.

Racking   Changing lenses by rotating the lens turret.

Remote   (n) A television production done outside the studio.

Roll cue   A transitional statement that enables a performer to yield to another segment of the program.

Splice   To mend, usually to cut out a portion and rejoin, the tape or film.

Stand by   Signal (either verbal or visual) given from the control room for silence in the studio before the start of a rehearsal or broadcast.

Strike   (1) To remove objects no longer needed in the program. (2) To take down scenery after the program.

Super   Putting one visual image on top of another (superimposing).

Switcher   A piece of equipment consisting of selection buttons and control levers (fader bars) that change the picture being recorded or transmitted; often used to refer to the person who operates the equipment. (See Chapter 9.)

Tally light   The small red light on camera indicating when that camera is on the air; also called *cue light*.

Tape   (n) Any of several strips of plastic cut in various gauges and coated for different purposes, such as recording sound and picture. (v) To record the program.

T.D.   Technical director

Telecine   *See* **film chain.**

TelePrompTer   A mechanical device that projects the moving script directly in front of the camera lens; a type of electronic "idiot card" that can be seen by the speaker but not by the audience.

Tilt Movement of the camera up or down while the mount remains stationary.

Truck Movement of the entire camera mount (pedestal) left or right.

Video The picture portion of the program.

Voice-over Narration which is read by an offscreen talent as silent film or tape footage is run on the screen.

VTR Video tape recorder or recording.

Wing it To do the program without a rehearsal.

Zoom A multipurpose lens that can change focal length in and out and near and far. Gives the effect of dollying without moving the camera. (v) To use a zoom lens.

A bit of advice before we leave the topic of studio language. As a novice, you should avoid trying to impress the production staff with your mastery of their language. We have seen many people come into the studio for the first time and try to speak the jargon of the television professional as a way of establishing that they are "one of the gang." In our experience, these attempts only produce negative results. Therefore, we suggest that you use the language of the studio only when you firmly understand that language.

Hand Signals

As we indicated a few pages ago, the language of the television studio is both verbal and nonverbal—and it behooves you to learn both languages if you expect to be successful as a television performer. Having introduced you to some of the words and phrases you will be exposed to in the studio, on pp. 93–96 we present some of the more common nonverbal messages with which you should be familiar.

In most instances many nonverbal messages will be given by the floor manager, who will be standing next to the camera you are to look at. Of course, there are going to be occasions when the production staff consists of you and the camera operator. But even in those instances, you should understand and use the following gestures.

Scripts

Whether you are preparing for an interview or designing your own program, a script is a means of coordinating the audio, visual, time, content, and human variables of television. When we introduce the topic of

FLOOR CUES

CUE	MEANING	DESCRIPTION
Stand by: 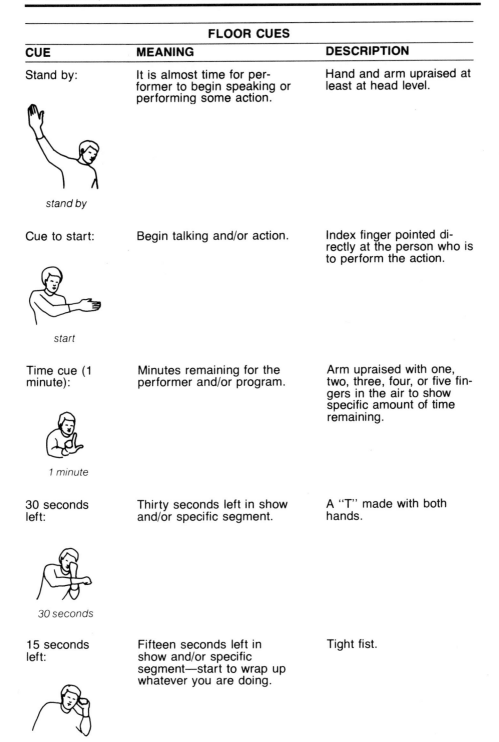 *stand by*	It is almost time for performer to begin speaking or performing some action.	Hand and arm upraised at least at head level.
Cue to start: *start*	Begin talking and/or action.	Index finger pointed directly at the person who is to perform the action.
Time cue (1 minute): *1 minute*	Minutes remaining for the performer and/or program.	Arm upraised with one, two, three, four, or five fingers in the air to show specific amount of time remaining.
30 seconds left: *30 seconds*	Thirty seconds left in show and/or specific segment.	A "T" made with both hands.
15 seconds left: *15 seconds*	Fifteen seconds left in show and/or specific segment—start to wrap up whatever you are doing.	Tight fist.

FLOOR CUES

CUE	MEANING	DESCRIPTION
Finish (wrap it up):	End the discussion and/or action.	Arm upraised with knuckles of fist pointed toward the performer.

wrap it up

Cut:	Stop talking and/or action.	Moving the hand across the throat in a cutting motion.

cut

Speed up:	Talk faster and/or skip some of your material—time is running out.	Rotating the index finger clockwise in circle—the faster the rotation the greater the need to speed up.

speed up

Slow down:	Slow down. Too much time remaining—ahead of schedule.	Hands are pulled apart in slow motion, as if pulling rubber bands.

slow down

OK:	Everything is going well—keep talking or engaging in your current action.	Circle made with the thumb and forefinger.

ok

FLOOR CUES

CUE	MEANING	DESCRIPTION
Back up:	Move back—too close to the camera.	Pushing motion with both hands.

back up

| Come closer: | Move closer to the camera. | Palms facing the person giving the cues; both hands moving toward the chest. |

come closer

| More volume: | Speak louder. | Cupping the ear with the hand. |

more volume

| Less volume: | Speak softer. | Raising palm to lips. |

less volume

FLOOR CUES

CUE	MEANING	DESCRIPTION
Speak to or look at a particular camera or microphone:	You should be looking at this camera or speaking into this microphone.	Hand pointing to a specific camera or microphone. A wave of that hand means get ready to move to another camera —it is about to be "activated."

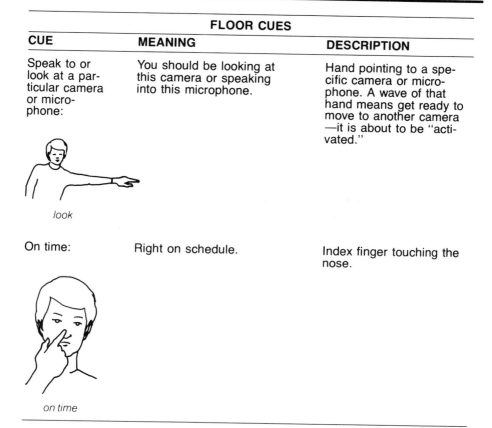

look

CUE	MEANING	DESCRIPTION
On time:	Right on schedule.	Index finger touching the nose.

on time

scripting to most novice performers, we usually get the same initial response: "I don't want to be an actor. I want to be natural and spontaneous when I appear on television." For them, the word *script* conjures up major dramatic productions in which actors perform memorized roles. While a script does contain the words of the show, it also includes much more—for instance, instructions about matters of production for members of the crew, enabling them to visualize how to integrate their specific responsibilities with the overall show. During rehearsal, the script also serves as guide for further alterations.

The amount of content contained in the script will vary from format to format. But regardless of the type of program, in rehearsal and during the program, all involved must know what is expected of them—and the script is the guide. It helps establish the show's organization, structure, and timing. As we noted, you can't be successful on television if you are poorly organized. The same is true of the entire production; it can't leap from point to point. The script helps all parties know the show's sequences—how it will begin, move, and conclude.

Different kinds of budget, personnel, and production format mean different kinds of scripts. Let us look at some scripts that you are likely to prepare or at least be exposed to.

DETAILED SCRIPTS   Plays, political talks, editorials, and even some news and talk shows call for detailed scripts. In these productions, nearly every word and picture is known in advance, written down, and controlled. Detailed scripts normally contain five types of information:

1. The spoken copy, be it a monologue or dialogue, written by you or someone else.

2. Notes and instructions for the production staff.

3. Musical information—when the theme music will begin, how long it will play, and when it will end. The musical portion of the script will also show if music is used during the various transitions needed in the program.

4. Major visual elements.

5. Miscellaneous production information. If there are sound effects, graphics, special tapes, set changes, and the like, it is necessary for everyone to have that data.

SEMI-SCRIPT   This document does not contain every word, note, and direction of the program—only the information needed for a given program. The partially scripted approach works well for interview programs, demonstrations, sportscasts, educational lecture shows, and other programs and formats where there is a great deal of ad-libbing. While many of these productions give the impression of being unstructured and spontaneous, they are not unprepared.

RUNDOWN SHEET   This type of script is used primarily in daily or weekly shows that employ the same format all the time: panel discussions, instructional-television lectures, regular interview programs, and other productions that seldom vary from show to show. The consistency of the format does not mean, however, that issues such as timing, organization, sequencing, movement, and the like can be left to chance. Quite the contrary: the rundown sheet takes care of them.

As you can see from this discussion, what a script is and how it is used varies from person to person and from program to program. How-

VIDEO	AUDIO	TIME
(a) The visual content of the program is described in this column:	(a) The audio portion of the program is described in this column--what is being said and by whom:	
Open with the logo of the station.		(:30)
	ANNC: Today our program examines the human effects of forest fires. Our guest is Fire Marshall Ray Jones.	(:45)
(b) Camera directions are given in this column:	(b) Special audio effects are noted in this column:	
Cut to a close-up (CU) of the talent.	Fire trucks and sirens are heard in the background.	(1:30)
(c) Special visual effects are noted in this column:	(c) Pretaped music and/or commercials are noted in this column:	
Run film of the fire.		
	Play program theme music.	

Figure 7.6 Sample elements found in most television scripts

ever, there are some features common to most television scripts. For example, most scripts are designed to clarify the visual, sound, and time-sequence components of a program. Figure 7.6 displays an example of the elements found in most scripts. (It is not a sample script; we will show you one of those on page 101.)

Preparing the Script

When you are preparing a script, you must ask yourself three questions: (1) Who is the audience that will be viewing me and the program? (2) Why is this production being put on the air? (3) How long should the script be? The answers will influence the content and length of your script. Let us briefly look at each of these questions and point out how they might actually influence your preparation.

The issue of *who* your audience is was treated in detail in Chapter 2. We noted that you must adapt your message to a *specific* audience. If you're talking about air pollution, you can't expect lay citizens watching a local talk show to know as much about the topic as a group of environmental engineers viewing a closed-circuit program aimed especially at them. In short, knowing your specific target is essential to preparing the script.

The *why* of the production and the reason for your appearance also need to be considered when preparing the script. For a weekly entertainment program, with many people on camera, your script must be brief and not full of serious information. On the other hand, for a fifteen-minute campaign speech, with you as the only speaker, your script will be detailed in both content and direction.

Finally, the amount of *airtime* for the program and the time allotted to you must also be taken into account. Obviously, a five-minute videotape prepared for company use does not employ the same script as a ninety-minute network program.

MANUSCRIPT MECHANICS   Some basic steps must be followed in preparing a script. The pages should be typed on only one side, double- or triple-spaced, and numbered in the upper right-hand corner. In some instances, each line is also numbered for easy reference. ("See page 4, line 17 for the changes in our opening shot.") Sentences should be completed on the same page on which they begin, to avoid having to flip the page in the middle of an idea.

Completed scripts must also show the timing of the program. The time allowed for each segment of the program—openings, camera movements, audio changes, dialogue, transitions, and endings—should appear in a column in the right-hand margin.

Finally, although it seems like a trivial point, pages of a script are *never* stapled together. It impedes the process of making changes during rehearsal.

MARKING THE SCRIPT   The marking and coding of the script is, in some ways, as important as the dialogue. Marking and coding alert the crew to what is expected of them.

All dialogue, and other "talk," is typed in upper and lower case. All audio cues (excluding speech), and music cues, are typed in capitals: CUE MUSIC. Directions to performers are in capital letters and enclosed in parentheses: (STAND UP AND GREET THE HOST). Video instructions use both capital letters and lowercase letters: CU, dolly in. Although no universal set of marks is used in preparing scripts, the following symbols seem to be the most popular:

---

(3) = Camera number three
< or FI = Fade in
SUP or S = Superimpose
T = Take

$\asymp$ or D = Dissolve
SD = Slow dissolve
\> or FO = Fade out
Q = Cue
PREP (2) = Prepare camera 2
DI = Dolly in
DB or DO = Dolly out
TC = Title card
2–sh = Shot of two persons
3–sh = Shot of three persons
O/S = Over-the-shoulder shot
CU = Closeup shot
MS = Medium shot
LS = Long shot
ECU or XCU = Tight closeup
MLS = Medium long shot
MCU = Medium closeup[3]

USING THE SCRIPT   In Part Five we will discuss in depth how you present your message. In this chapter, however, we are concerned with the script as a technical part of the studio experience. It is possible for you to read directly from the script, but we recommend that you avoid this mode of delivery. It tends to be overly formal and makes you appear to be more interested in the script than in the audience. If, however, you have to use your 8½ × 11 piece of paper, try to follow these guidelines:

1. Type on blue or green paper if the audience is going to see the script (as we will point out later, the camera reacts unfavorably to most other colors).

2. Remember to use eye contact with the camera—don't just look at your script.

3. Make sure the script is easy to read.

Some performers prefer to read from 5 × 7 cards. These cards, whether they be yours or someone else's, should be blue or green, numbered, and clear.

The entire script, or parts of it, can be transferred to **cue cards** (often called "idiot cards"), large poster boards (14 × 22 inches) that are held near the "on" camera. They are easy to see and, as you get used to them, help you convey the impression that you are talking directly to the audience.

Finally, the script, or portions of it, can be placed on a Tele-PrompTer. This device, which will be discussed again in Part Five, is attached to the front of the camera. The prepared copy is projected onto a glass plate directly in front of the lens. This particular method of dealing with your script is hard to master (your eyes tend to track, left to right, which looks strange); however, with practice it can be very effective.

The following script is an example of a typical format showing how the video, audio, and time columns are commonly treated. The script, written by one of our students, was designed for a three-minute presentation, and calls for the use of three cameras.

This script follows the motivated sequence discussed in Part Three ("Structuring Television Messages"). It represents a persuasive intent: A problem is identified, solutions are visualized, and action is hoped for on the part of the viewer.

Hospices: Death Traps or Havens on Earth

by Sheryl Chenin

VIDEO	AUDIO	TIME
Camera 2 fade up MS. Roll character generator with title.	Hospices: Death Traps or Havens on Earth.	:10
Camera 2 zoom to CU of speaker.	Today there are three main kinds of care available for the terminally ill: hospitals, nursing homes, and hospices. Of the three, only the hospice is aimed at meeting the needs of both the patients and their families.	:20
Cut to Camera 3: MS of speaker.	Because hospices work strictly with terminal patients, a lot of time is spent teaching the patients how to cope with death, and their survivors how to cope with life.	:25
Dissolve to Camera 2: CU of speaker.	A relatively new idea in the United States, hospice care is often misunderstood. During the next few minutes I will tell you: (1) some common misconceptions; (2) how to change these views; and (3) what this would	:45

VIDEO	AUDIO	TIME
	mean to terminal patients and their families. Finally, I will tell you what you can do to help.	
Dissolve to Camera 3: MS.	Most of the misconceptions about hospices stem from the knowledge that they deal with death. According to a list of major obstacles that was presented to the Third National Hospice Symposium in San Rafael, California, "Problems are created by the fact that death and dying is a taboo subject that arouses many personal and cultural fears."	:60
Cut to Camera 2: CU of speaker.	Other problems exist because hospices are seen as death traps from which no one ever returns home. This could not be further from the truth.	1:05
	Knowing that 76 percent of all terminal patients wish to die at home, most hospices not only provide a homelike environment but also find a way for many patients to return home for their last days.	1:15
Dissolve to Camera 3: MS of speaker.	Another misconception occurs because euthanasia and hospices are often confused. Although both are dedicated to relieving pain and suffering, hospice programs do nothing to hasten a person's death.	1:25
Cut to MS Camera 3; slow zoom to CU.	Perhaps the best way to understand life in a hospice is through someone who has seen death there. Sidney G. Reeman was a patient who died March 3, 1975, in a hospice. Like many, before he died, he started writing poetry. One of the poems, "In the Midst of Life," said, "Here in this hospice I can truly say that death has been met with dignity."	1:45
Dissolve to Camera 2: MS.	As for changing the way hospices are viewed, the only way to ac-	2:00

VIDEO	AUDIO	TIME
	complish this great task is through education. By demonstrating that hospice work is practical and beneficial to the patients, their families, and the working staff, it will become a more acceptable form of patient care.	
Camera 3: MS.	What this would mean to terminal patients and their families is a better availability of hospice programs for those who desire their services.	2:05
Camera 2: MS.	Rather than fear it, we should recognize the hospice as a civilized means to meet death with dignity.	2:10
Camera 2 zoom to CU.	In closing, I would like to urge each of you to keep your mind open, even to things you don't understand. Through education, misconceptions can be dispelled and attitudes changed.	2:20
Camera 3: MS.	For those of you who would like more information, I would recommend calling the Nathan Adelson Hospice here in Las Vegas at 733-0320. Another good source of information is the public library.	2:35
Camera 2: MS.	The library has many books on this subject including: The Hospice Way of Death by Paul M. Dubois, A Hospice Handbook: A New Way to Care for the Dying, edited by Michael P. Hamilton and Helen F. Reid, and New Meanings of Death by Herman Feifel.	2:50
Camera 1: Fade up color slide of a beautiful, sunny mountain meadow. Roll character generator with title.	I suggest you do some research and try to keep in mind the words of Bacclylides, "Hardest of deaths to a mortal/Is the death he sees ahead." Hospices might make that death easier.	3:00

REHEARSALS

Now that you know something about the people of television, and their verbal, nonverbal, and written language, you should be ready to learn about *your* role in the production, starting with what you do during the rehearsal period.

Rehearsals, like so many elements of television production, take a variety of forms. Whether the rehearsal is brief or extended, involves many people or a few, depends on such things as the purpose and complexity of the program, the budget, the experience of the talent, the type of studio, time constraints, and whether the program is shot on location or in the studio.

Regardless of format, all rehearsals are carried out for two reasons: to practice the production prior to the taping, and to make any necessary improvements. To accomplish these purposes, most rehearsals are divided into three sessions: pre-studio rehearsals, run-throughs, and dress rehearsals.

Pre-Studio Rehearsals

Pre-studio rehearsals usually involve two phases: first, a series of meetings that take place before anyone moves into the studio, followed by the production team's preparation of the studio.

REHEARSAL MEETINGS   Because studio time is costly and precious, most directors try to have some meetings outside the studio before the first working rehearsal. These meetings serve to let the production crew get to know each other, introduce staff members to the show's script and purpose, and provide an opportunity to discuss production questions such as equipment, facilities, blocking, sound, and camera sequencing. Our experience has shown us that these meetings are most beneficial when everyone comes prepared and takes an active role.

TECHNICAL REHEARSAL   While the next phase is often referred to as a pre-studio rehearsal, it is actually a rehearsal without performers—but in the studio. The production crew uses this time to get the set ready by bringing in props, arranging furniture, chalking and taping the floor, practicing blocking and camera shots, and getting a rough idea of timing.

As is the case in all three steps of the rehearsal period, the director will discuss and recommend the changes he or she deems necessary.

Figure 7.7
In this technical rehearsal the host is not in costume, and a member of the staff stands in for the guest, allowing the crew to adjust sound and light levels ahead of time. Photography by Scott Highton. Courtesy of Over Easy/KQED.

Run-Through Rehearsal

In this phase of rehearsal, the performer begins to take a more active role. You are asked to go through your movements, sit or stand in the spot you will occupy during the performance, and work on your lines. This enables you and the director to become familiar with your part and analyze areas of improvement. All this is going on while the technical aspects of the program—lighting, sound, special effects, timing, camera sequencing—are being refined. If you had planned to move to one side of the set, for example, and now discover you would be out of camera range, the necessary modifications are made.

Don't be surprised if you are asked to perform the same action repeatedly: Although it involves a great many and tedious stops and starts, as problems arise and are resolved, this period is crucial to the success of the production. We should note, however, that the type of program (talk show or dramatic), and the complexity of the production (one camera or ten) will help determine how many times some action is repeated.

Dress Rehearsal

The dress rehearsal is the last rehearsal before the actual production. In this rehearsal, the complete production will not be interrupted unless there is a serious problem. All suggestions are withheld until the rehearsal is completed, when everyone meets to discuss what has taken place. In most instances, major alterations are kept to a minimum.

Rehearsal and the Speaker

The following procedures and techniques can help the speaker make the television experience a successful one.

1. *Be punctual.* If you are tardy, you will be keeping a great many people waiting, which means a considerable amount of money will be wasted. During the years when we hosted a talk show, we would even ask our guests to arrive early so that they could get the feel of the studio. This early arrival also allows time for makeup to be applied.

    In arranging your schedule around a rehearsal, allot plenty of time. Some rehearsals take a long time. Pacing up and down because you have another appointment can be disconcerting to the other members of the crew.

2. *Adopt a relaxed and courteous manner.* Although you might be nervous and somewhat confused by the new environment, you should still try to remain calm and cheerful. The other members of the production team will find you easier to work with, and most likely will help you more, if you have a positive attitude.

3. *Be ready to explain any special features of your presentation.* Before the rehearsal begins is the time to let the director know if you need any special equipment, visual aids, props, wardrobe, and the like.

4. *Keep the floor manager informed of your whereabouts during the rehearsal.* If you're needed for an important sequence, but have gone for a walk, the entire production crew has to wait for your return. Therefore, either ask to leave or wait until you're dismissed.

5. *Be prepared.* Knowing your part is crucial if the rehearsal and production are to go well. People don't want to stop while you learn your lines.

Figure 7.8

It's always important to be prepared, whether you are a guest making your first appearance on television or a seasoned professional. Here a host is reviewing the script with production assistants.

6. *Become familiar with possible mistakes.* Learn to overcome the four most common production errors performers make during rehearsal:

    a. Being out of position—off the assigned marks or in the wrong place

    b. Facing the wrong camera—forgetting to look for the camera with the tally light (red light) on

    c. Forgetting dialogue or saying the wrong dialogue—freezing up or misreading cue cards or TelePrompTer

    d. Poor appearance on camera—wrong clothes, inappropriate makeup, and so on

7. *Learn to ask questions.* As we have noted throughout this chapter, too many novice performers let the experience of being in the studio intimidate them. Don't let the studio get in the way of your doing a good job. Be polite, yet assertive. And don't be afraid to ask questions. What follows is a partial list of the types of questions you should ask. The answers to these and other questions will enable you to have a much clearer idea of what is expected of you as you get ready to make your appearance on television.

a. How long will I have for my presentation?

b. Will the program be live or recorded? (You can stop and edit a recorded program; rehearsal and serious preparation become even more important when your performance is live.)

c. Will I have access to films, props, or other audiovisual aids? (Ask this well in advance of the production, so that you can assemble your own supporting material if necessary.)

d. Who else will be on camera with me?

e. Will I have cue cards, a TelePrompTer, or my own cards?

f. What kinds of cues will the director be using? (While most directors and floor managers employ the cues we have discussed, you should nevertheless verify this point.)

g. How many cameras will be used? Will an overhead boom or lavaliere microphone be used?

SUMMARY

Even when you are working with a minimum of television equipment, we recommend that several people work together. You may not work with all of the people we have discussed in this chapter, or you may be working with more; in either case, our point is that good television presentations reflect the labors of several people. Knowing those people and their abilities is important.

It's also important to share the language of the people you work with. The vocabulary, gestures, and scripting that we describe in this chapter do not cover the complete language of the studio, but it should provide a basis for adequate communication.

8. PRIMARY TELEVISION HARDWARE

Learning something about the staff and the specialized language they use is only the first step in overcoming studio anxiety. Recognizing and understanding the equipment you will be facing is equally important. If you know what the equipment can do, you'll be able to use it to advantage; you won't feel bewildered and intimidated as a camera moves ominously toward you and a microphone boom dangles precariously over your head.

We've divided television equipment into two categories. The camera and the microphone—equipment most directly related to the speaker —are deemed primary. Secondary television equipment—recorders, switchers, and editors—will be discussed in the next chapter.

CAMERAS

Communicating in front of a camera is an art, one that necessitates at least a rudimentary understanding of camera types, shots, and movements, three factors that will influence how the viewers perceive you and subsequently respond to your message. (Operating a video camera is an art in itself, one treated at greater length in the readings recommended at the end of this part.)

Types of Cameras

We classify television cameras according to portability, color capability, and expense. Each classification provides information about a camera that can make the difference between effective or ineffective use of television.

PORTABLE VS. NONPORTABLE   A portable unit is excellent for location interviews, home practice, and "home movies." High-quality portable units can be used successfully for internal company communications; they also bring us the field reports on the evening news. But, as of this

Figure 8.1 Portable camera

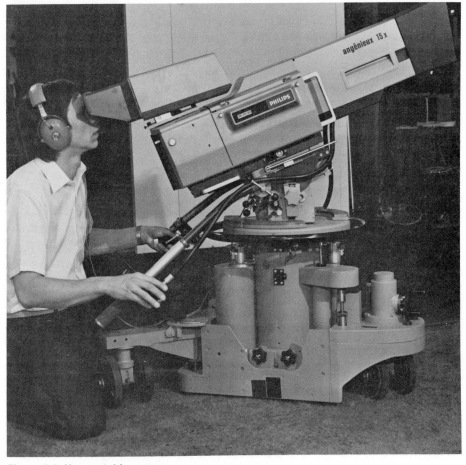

Figure 8.2 Nonportable camera

writing, a portable camera will not produce network-quality video. The commercial network television that is most familiar to us is produced with nonportable cameras.

   One of the key differences between portable and nonportable units is that the latter have a tally light that indicates when the camera is on the air. With portable equipment you must depend on cues from the camera operator. Not having a tally light can lead to confusion, if not disaster. One author went through the embarrassing experience of watching a broadcast interview done earlier that included material taped before he thought the camera was on and after he thought the camera was off. There was no real harm done, but such a situation could conceivably have serious consequences.

When working in a studio, you will have to learn how to use the tally light. In a studio where there are two or three cameras, the switcher (discussed in detail in the next chapter) may cut or fade from one camera to another. Unless you make a corresponding change in the direction of your gaze, you are suddenly caught looking at something other than your audience. (However, if you are leading in to a visual other than yourself, a shot of your profile looking at something other than your audience would be preferable.)

Two situations in particular seem to confuse novices most: when the light changes to another camera, and when two lights are on at the same time. If there are two cameras and the tally light goes off on one, then you know you should turn your attention to the other camera. But if you have three cameras aimed at you, you may have trouble following a change from one camera to another. You may find yourself searching, feeling and looking awkward. Professional television speakers have developed the skill of turning gracefully from one camera to another, dropping their eyes when the tally light goes off (as if checking their notes), then locating the tally light through peripheral vision. Then they come up from their notes to the right camera.

When two lights are on at the same time, the switcher is usually making a fade from one camera to another. You will know that the camera you have been looking at is going to go off, so you can smoothly change your gaze to the new light.

At most professional studios, a floor manager will wave you from one camera to another. But if you're working in a studio that is short on staff, your understanding of the tally light could make the difference between good and poor eye contact with your audience.

COLOR VS. BLACK-AND-WHITE Whether to use color or black-and-white cameras depends on the nature of the presentation. Black-and-white equipment is excellent for home practice, videotape training, surveillance, and documentaries or docudramas.

However, we prefer color over black-and-white cameras for two reasons. First, as we point out in Part Five, color in dress, skin tone, and scenery has a significant impact on the effectiveness of television communication. Second, a color camera is more versatile: If you need black-and-white coverage, you can get it with a color camera—but you will never get color with black-and-white.

COST If you're interested only in home practice, an inexpensive camera can be a valuable tool—something you can use with your home recorder and television set. Producing images of network quality, however, requires a sizable outlay.

You gain some control over your television presentation by understanding the types of cameras available. For example, if you are asked to do an interview for a local television station, you may have the choice of portable or studio cameras. It doesn't hurt to ask, and a portable unit may enable you to demonstrate your point in a way that would be impossible with a nonportable camera in hard-to-reach locations.

Camera Shots

Controlling your television image requires an understanding of camera shots as well as of camera types. Camera shots are generally designated by distance or anatomy.

You need to know about five common distance shots to describe what you want captured by the eye of the camera (see Figure 8.3).

The terms describe the distance a speaker has between self and camera and, to some degree, the distance between self and audience. The initials are used in scripts as a means of letting everyone involved in the production process know what is expected.

Camera shots are also described in anatomical terms (see Figure 8.4).

Camera Mountings and Movements

Understanding camera mounting is prologue to understanding camera movement. A television camera has five possible mountings. **Hand-held** cameras are particularly difficult to hold steady. **Shoulder-mounted** cameras give the operator greater stability since they rest on the shoulder, are held by the hand, and may rest against the hand. The shoulder-mounted camera brings us a good portion of the evening news.

A **tripod-mounted** camera rests on three legs and may swivel at the top and have a modicum of height adjustment. A tripod dolly is a tripod with casters on its feet. A tripod allows the camera operator complete stability, but limits mobility.

A studio pedestal involves a base and one central shaft topped by the camera. A **pedestal mount** allows greater up-and-down motion but is generally stationary (see Figure 8.5).

Human, tripod, and pedestal mounting are the most common in television work. However, most professional studios will also have **crane mounts.** A crane-mounted camera takes a lot of room, but frees the camera for a great deal of movement. It can look down on a scene in a way not possible with other cameras.

On each of these mounts, the camera may **pan**—horizontally scan—the scene. Each also allows for a **tilt-vertical scanning.** The whole camera may also be moved; up-and-down movement is called

Framing	Step	Symbol
	Extreme Long Shot	XLS or ELS
	Long Shot	LS
	Medium Shot	MS
	Close-up	CU
	Extreme Close-up	XCU or ECU

Figure 8.3 Common distance shots

Framing	Step	Symbol	
	Bust Shot	Bust Shot	(shows upper torso and head)
	Knee Shot	Knee Shot	(from the knee up)
	Two-Shot (two persons in frame)	2-Shot	
	Three-Shot (three persons in frame)	3-Shot	
	Over-the-Shoulder Shot	O-S	(if taken to a closeup, gives the appearance of one person being seen through the eyes of another)

Figure 8.4 Camera shots described in anatomical terms

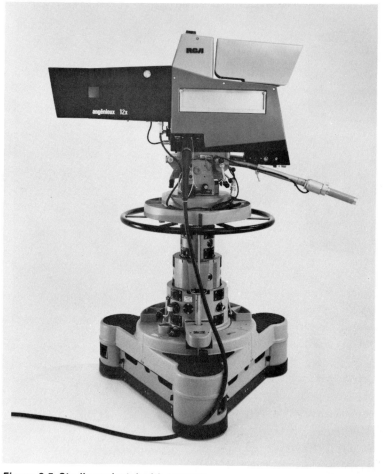

Figure 8.5 Studio pedestal with camera

pedestal movement and back-and-forth movement is called **dolly movement.**

A fifth type of movement is independent of the camera's mounting. A **zoom lens** makes it possible to zoom in and out of the focus of attention.

Movement gives television the illusion of life. Alistair Cooke once said that the "camera loves action." The camera also lends action to video presentations through pan, tilt, pedestal, dolly, and zoom movement.

As the preceding discussion has indicated, we think that the camera is a critical component of television communications, the one that best bridges the space between the technical and the human variables of television communication. However, although the camera is the most obvious piece of equipment in a studio, it is only one part of an electronic complex.

MICROPHONES

Because so much emphasis is placed on the visual dimension of television, the importance of sound is often overlooked. But the audience hears you as well as sees you, so you should know something about sound equipment, particularly microphones. The equipment needed to convert the sound of the studio to someone's television set is complex. The cables, wires, turntables, consoles, signal processors, loudspeakers, and the like are far beyond the scope of this book. Nonetheless, you can improve your effectiveness on television by learning about various types of microphones and some techniques for using them.

A production involving music and/or speeches calls for one kind of microphone. Outdoor (remote) locations require another kind. Familiarity with the choices available should improve the effectiveness of your presentation. You can supplement this information with additional reading and by talking with audio experts.

Types of Microphones

All microphones are alike in that they convert sound waves (produced by voices, music, special effects, and so on) into electrical current. This current is amplified and reconverted into sound waves that can be projected from a loudspeaker. Microphones differ in their construction and their usage. If this book had been written for television technicians, we would explain both of these classifications. However, since our concern is with the performing aspects of television, we will examine how six of the most common microphones are used, not constructed. While new technology is constantly improving television audio, the following six types of microphones seem to endure.

HAND MICROPHONE   As the name implies, the hand microphone is held by the performer. It is quite useful in remote broadcasts, interviews, audience-participation shows, and one-person productions. As you would suspect, having to hold the microphone limits your range of movement and gestures. There must be enough cable to allow you to move around while keeping the cable out of sight; with one hand holding the microphone, you either have to gesture with one hand or move the microphone around without losing sound.

There is yet another problem with using a hand-held microphone: Because of the rough treatment these microphones receive, they must be durable and rugged; this in turn limits the quality of sound they produce. Although they are not 100 percent effective, you may want to use a windscreen when recording out of doors. These screens, or filters, can be adapted to most microphones and can reduce some of the distortion from blowing wind or excessive hand movements.

DESK MICROPHONE   Very popular in panel discussions, lectures, political speeches, and other situations where people are seated behind or around a table, the desk microphone gives access to more than one person. Desk microphones are extremely sensitive: You should be aware of the extraneous noises you might make if you were to rattle your script or tap your fingers on the table.

STAND MICROPHONE   Simply a hand or desk microphone that is placed on a floor stand, the stand mike enables you to have both hands free. Of course, like the desk microphone, it limits your mobility range.

Figure 8.6 Stand microphone

LAVALIERE MICROPHONE   The lavaliere mike has become a very popular model in recent years, for good reasons. First, because the lavaliere microphone is very small it can be clipped to a blouse, shirt, or lapel, or hung around the neck on a thin cord. Second, the lavaliere does not require a multitude of audio engineers or sophisticated facilities. You or the floor manager attaches the microphone, a volume check is taken, and the program is ready to begin. In talk shows featuring nonprofessionals, you can see how the ease of these three steps would be appreciated by both performers and crew. Third, since it's close to your mouth (approximately six inches below the chin), there is little chance for extraneous noise to be picked up.

Fourth, because the microphone is attached to a long, trailing wire, or plugged into a small personal transmitter, you can, within limits, move freely.

The lavaliere is not without its drawbacks, however. Because the lavaliere is basically used for voice pickup, it is not very effective in elaborate productions, musical shows, or other programs that demand a high quality of sound. And the size of the lavaliere makes it easy to

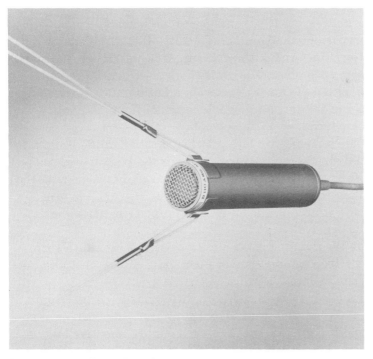

Figure 8.7 Lavaliere microphone

damage. Furthermore, it can pick up heavy breathing or the rubbing of clothing against the instrument. It is a good idea to practice with the lavaliere (or any microphone, for that matter) before the program begins. The lavaliere is also not very efficient for programs involving a great many people. As the various performers move their heads from side to side, engaging in conversation with others, they are apt to lose sound if they turn too far away from their personalized microphone.

Finally, the lavaliere takes time to get on and off. This means that it usually has to be attached before the program begins. Note that it must be attached *securely*. If you are part of a small production that doesn't have a floor manager, this will be your responsibility. We have observed, on many occasions, improperly fastened lavalieres clattering to the floor while the cameras were rolling.

BOOM MICROPHONE The boom takes many different forms, but basically it is a microphone that is attached to the end of a pipe or an adjustable extension pole. It can be hand-held, like a fishing pole; placed on a dolly that can be pushed around the studio; or set on a tripod. In all cases it has the advantage of being able to be circled or tilted as it records the sounds of the program.

There are, of course, other advantages to the boom microphone. You don't have to worry as much about being heard—the boom follows you from location to location. And with some larger booms, those locations can be distant from each other. Many directors also like the boom because it can be kept out of camera range. In addition, it doesn't require cables on the floor of the set. Audio engineers like the high-quality sound the boom produces.

Like all the microphones we have discussed thus far, the boom also has some potential shortcomings. First, it needs more personnel to operate it than the other microphones we have looked at. Someone is needed to hold and/or guide the boom toward the speaker. If a dolly is used, someone must move it around the studio. So in terms of personnel and equipment, it is expensive.

Second, while the fishing-pole boom may not take up much room, the dolly and the tripod demand lots of floor space. In small studios, or on location, this can be a problem.

Third, when a boom is used, special lighting has to be taken into consideration. If the crew isn't careful, shadows from the boom will appear on the screen. Finally, while the boom is highly sensitive and has a large pickup range, it can't cover the audio of people who are sitting or standing far apart. Therefore it has to be operated in a restricted area.

Figure 8.8
*Note the boom microphone hanging above the speaker
—and well above camera range.*

WIRELESS MICROPHONE   Perhaps you have noticed Phil Donahue or gameshow hosts carrying what appears to be just a long stick or wand as they walk around and sometimes off the stage into the audience. This stick is a wireless microphone, the newest type of microphone to be found in the studio. It has an amplifier, transmitter, batteries for these two devices, and even a transmitting antenna, all of which can be built directly into the unit or hidden on the performer. Although such equipment is expensive, it is unbeatable in those instances where stringing long cables is impractical.

Using the Microphone

In Part Five, "Presenting Yourself on Television," the way you speak into the microphone will be addressed. Yet we believe there are some technical aspects of the microphone that relate to your overall effectiveness as a communicator. Sound checks help assure clear audio reception, so be attentive when taking them. There are a few do's and don'ts in taking sound checks that you should be aware of:

1. Make sure the audio engineer lets you take more than one check. Because of your nervousness, the first two checks may not represent the real you.

2. Try to use your normal voice when taking the audio check. Don't mumble, yell, whisper, or try to sound like a professional newscaster—be yourself.

3. Don't take your check by saying "Testing one, two, three." This is the way you count, not the way you talk.

4. When taking the check, sit or stand in the same place you will be in during the actual performance. Taking the check sitting down and then giving your actual talk standing up will not provide an accurate voice-level reading.

Keep in mind that the microphone is a delicate instrument. Learn to treat it with great care. The personnel in the studio will regard you with more respect if you don't toss it, tap on it, or blow into it. These three behaviors, the ones novice performers seem to like the most, harm the instrument and your credibility.

We would advise you not to adjust the microphone—especially in a unionized studio. You are not a sound expert; furthermore, you don't belong to the union. If you get too close to or too far away from the microphone, let someone else reposition you and it. This suggestion does not apply, of course, if you are part of a very small production and serving as technician as well as performer.

Some microphones are engineered to pick up all sound, not just the sound you want it to. This means you must be aware of all distracting noises in the environment—those you produce as well as those generated by other sources. In a sense, the list of extraneous sounds in a studio is endless. However, there are a number of sounds you should avoid: coughing, breathing heavily, walking heavily, tapping your fingers, shuffling papers, whispering to someone off camera, shifting in your chair, rattling jewelry, and bumping into the microphone. Be cognizant of the simple fact that the microphone does not decide what it will broadcast; it can't discriminate—you must.

Take care not to place yourself too close to the microphone, especially when using a hand-held one. Beginning speakers have a tendency to act as if they plan to eat the microphone. Leaning forward not only looks awkward, and is unnecessary, but can distort how you sound. Microphones are engineered and audio checks established for you to be about six to ten inches from the instrument. Anything closer than that will distort your voice.

Finally, when using a lavaliere microphone, wear the wires, whenever possible, under your outer garments. The less conspicuous the wires, the more attractive your appearance on the screen.

SUMMARY

The camera and the microphone are the basic visual and auditory tools of television. We have explained the camera in terms of types, shots, and movements, and the microphone in terms of types and uses. Anyone seriously considering the use of television should learn the basic attributes of these primary tools.

9. SECONDARY TELEVISION HARDWARE

As you look around a professional television studio, you'll notice that the cameras and microphones are linked to an incredible array of apparatus. High-quality television production requires many secondary tools. We call them *secondary* not because they are less important, but because their use follows the use of the camera and the microphone. Our descriptions of this equipment will not be detailed; we realize that if your business is in front of the camera, you may never have to use a recorder or a switcher. However, the secondary hardware of a studio does affect the look and sound of a production and warrants at least rudimentary understanding by anyone involved in television communication.

We don't mention all the secondary television tools in this chapter—only the ones we think are particularly important. We will discuss **recorders** because they are particularly useful in home or small-business television production and because the recorder is as common a television tool as the camera or microphone; **switchers** because they are central to any professional studio and because they have such a significant effect on the final product; **character generators** and **editors** because they are necessary for sophisticated television production. Finally, we will discuss *visuals* as important tools of the television studio.

RECORDERS

The desire to preserve special moments and experiences is not new. Nearly two thousand years ago, Martial remarked: "To be able to enjoy one's past life is to live twice." The video recorder gives us that second life.

For millions of years, human memory has been the basic recorder. Wood, stone, metal, and paint have also been used to commemorate events. If television is the language of the twentieth century, then video recorders are the basic recording devices of the twentieth century.

Types of Recorders

The clearest division of video recorders is based on tape size. There are five basic sizes: ¼, ½, ¾, 1, and 2 inches. Sizes less than 1″ are considered "small format"; greater than 1″ are considered "large format." One-inch videotape is in the middle range.

Tape size is generally related to quality (and expense) in television production. The ¼″ size is bottom-of-the-line; 2″ is broadcast quality. The ¼″ size has its uses because of its economy. The popular ½″ size is designed for most home enthusiasts. The ¾″ and 1″, because of their affordability, are favored by most small businesses, universities, interest groups, artists, and others.

There are two common ½″ videotape systems: BETA and VHS. The differences between the two systems involve quality and duration of recording time. There is also a third ½″ system, which will produce broadcast-quality recordings. The BETACAM, a one-unit camera and video recorder, is a ½″ system, but because of different speeds and superior electronics, the BETACAM will not reproduce on a home BETA or VHS system. BETACAM tape must be replayed through a time base corrector (an expensive piece of equipment), and BETACAM units themselves are expensive (between $35,000 and $50,000).

If you are even remotely considering the use of television, we recommend ½″ tape as a means to an inexpensive home studio: ¼ and ½″ cameras are low-priced, and ¼ and ½″ tape can be edited. If you're using a commercial studio, you will be dealing with BETACAM, 1″, or 2″ tape. If you're interested in commercial or public exposure, we recommend that you work with ¾″, 1″, or 2″ videotape.

Advantages

The principle of videotape recording is quite simple: The electronic impulses of pictures and sound are recorded on a special magnetic tape, which can be played back later. There are, as you would suspect, a number of advantages to a system that would let you record, view, analyze, and store your message before and/or after you send it. You might want to think about a few of these advantages so that you can decide how to employ the recorder.

The most obvious advantage to videotape is that it can be shown to the audience at a time other than when it was first recorded. This allows for more convenient and efficient scheduling for both viewer and performer. The program can be shown at a time that is deemed best for the particular audience—be it the network news or a tape that has been prepared for a company party. Performers, whether they're being paid or not, appreciate being asked to appear when it is convenient for them. This flexibility in scheduling, made possible by videotape, has changed the whole look of television: We were once part of a weekly interview program that was recorded after ten o'clock at night, the only time everyone could be there, and broadcast on Sunday mornings.

Because some of the equipment used in videotaping is lightweight and highly mobile, it's very useful in remote programming. It lets the production staff plan shows that don't have to be confined to a studio. Courtrooms, offices, streets, and the like all become potential studios.

The most important advantage of videotape to the speaker is that it provides another chance. If you don't like what was done the first, second, or third time, it can be erased. Knowing that the entire sequence can be done again if you make a mistake alleviates a great deal of pressure. Videotape gives meaning to the cliché "If at first you don't succeed, ..."

Because tape allows for immediate playback, it is extremely useful as a learning tool; you can see yourself as a communicator *before* others see you. From eye contact to organizational skills, you can watch and listen to what others will finally watch and listen to. The recorder can be a highly personal piece of equipment. The tape can be shown in private on a one-viewer-per-screen device. The instant rerun lets you make the necessary adjustments.

Disadvantages

Every advantage that we mention can also be a disadvantage. The fact that a tape can be shown at any time means that the context of time is removed from the presentation. What if you're interviewed today, but your presentation isn't shown for two years? Often what we say today sounds foolish tomorrow. Most experienced performers are aware of this potential problem and therefore try to formulate their remarks in light of the future of the program. If they believe that the tape will be shown over and over (and year after year), they'll make the necessary adjustments in their use of examples and evidence. In short, they avoid references that date the program.

Erasure and editing are advantages in video recording, if you are the one erasing and editing your own presentation. As we have found out the hard way, when someone else edits and erases, the results are not always to our advantage. For example, when the local superintendent of public education speaks to the teachers of the public school system through closed circuit television, there is one recording of his presentation, and he has that one recording. His address might be different if he were talking to the teachers and staff through recordings passed out to each teacher and staff member.

SWITCHERS

The switcher, one of the more intriguing-looking pieces of equipment in the studio, contains rows of multicolored buttons (often lighted) and fader bars. Perhaps more than any other television tool, the switcher manifests the look of control.

There are generally at least four rows (**buses**) of buttons on a video switcher: a **preview** row that enables the technical director, director, or producer, at the push of a button, to see the picture before it goes on the air; two rows of **mix** buses, each controlling one particular video input; and a row of **program** buses, buttons that determine what goes out of the studio either on tape or on the air.

The **fader bars** are leverlike controls that enable the operator to fade from one bus position to another. If you have two cameras set up, one can be feeding one bus, the other another bus. To cut from one camera image to another, you simply press one bus, then the other. With a fader bar, you can dissolve from one image to another by overlapping two buses.

A switcher allows you to go from one video source to another. You might have two or three cameras, a film chain, and perhaps a slide or two feeding into the switcher. Between the buses and fader bars, you can move to and from the various inputs in four basic ways: the cut, the dissolve, the fade, and the wipe.

The **cut** is an instant change from one image to another; it occurs with a change of bus. The **dissolve** is a gradual transition from one image to another, with the two images overlapping for a period of time determined by the director. A **fade** is a transition from one segment to another by using black (no picture) in place of one of the cameras. Thus a fade-in is actually a dissolve from black to a camera shot, while a fade-out is a dissolve from a camera that is "on" to black. A **wipe** pushes one image off the screen while replacing it with another picture. There are a number of wipes that can be employed. Two of the most common are the horizontal wipe, which pushes off one shot and replaces it (like sliding a door), and the vertical wipe, which gives the impression of a window shade moving up or down.

The cut, dissolve, fade, and wipe movements produced with a switcher function as transitions in a video presentation; they are used as directions in a script, and can be viewed as forms of instant editing that allow you to move from one picture source to another.

The switcher is as complex as it sounds. With the buses and fader bars a director can cut, dissolve, fade, and wipe different images produced by different cameras and different visual sources. This instant editing can make or ruin a program. You may never be called upon to use a switcher, but its ability to change the nature of a video presentation makes it an important piece of equipment—one that must be understood if you are interested in controlling the medium of television.

EDITORS

Editors give you the flexibility of selecting the best footage for your presentation. They let you add to or subtract from the original tape: You can edit out what does not add to your presentation and edit in what does. (If you're working in a professional studio, you and the director can edit the material together.)

Video editing is complex. One videotape is run and new material is added—without cutting the tape. There are two ways the editing process commonly works. You can have a blank master tape on which you place shots selected from other videotapes; or you can have one tape with material on it, and insert material from another tape.

To edit, you need several pieces of video equipment: the editor itself and two recorders (a playback machine that shows visuals and a second recorder that tapes them together). When you press the edit button for the playback machine, subsequent material is erased from the master tape and replaced with the new material from the second playback machine.

Figure 9.1 The editor

Good editing starts with the planning of a presentation, continues during the taping, and is continued after the taping is finished. A polished video presentation reflects critical thinking and continuous editing.

If you're considering a home studio, you'll find the editor to be one of the more expensive video tools. In small-format television (1″ or less tape size), the editing equipment is affordable. A ½″ editor is feasible for most individuals. A ¾″ editor is within easy reach of most organizations. If you're interested in competing with the quality of commercial television, an editor is necessary. It can make the difference between the amateur and professional production.

CHARACTER GENERATORS

At the beginning of some television programs, and at the end of others, the credits—the names of the director, producer, and other people involved in the program—are displayed on the screen in clean, clear, standardized lettering. In most cases, that lettering is made on a character generator.

A character generator is something like a word processor in that it has a keyboard, a screen, and the ability to store a message, to be used whenever the director so desires. The message typed on a character generator goes to the switcher. The director can use a bus or a fader bar to bring the credits on line.

The character generator can enliven the video image in two basic ways. First, the credits can be *rolled,* that is, moved from the top to the bottom or the bottom to the top of the screen. A character generator can also *crawl* a message across the screen, from left to right or from right to left.

If you like typewriters and use a typewriter as a tool, you will find the character generator to be one of the easiest tools to adapt to in the television studio. Like all the tools of television presentation, the character generator lends versatility to the presentation and can make the difference between a clear message and a muddied one.

VISUALS

Visuals—graphic materials, photographs, slides, films, and three-dimensional objects—are valuable in any television presentation. They arouse and hold attention; they help support main points; they can add clarity to your message. To communicate effectively on television, you need to know about the special requirements and the types of visuals, and how to use them.

Special Requirements

DIMENSIONS   An important criterion in selecting aids centers around the idea of **aspect ratio.** Television pictures are always in a format of three units high and four units wide, so all pictures, graphs, and so on, should be presented in a 3:4 ratio. Otherwise they'll be cut off if too big and look awkward if they fall below this ratio.

Obviously it is impossible to have pictures, graphs, charts, and the like meet the exact ratio requirements. Therefore, try to allow a border of one-sixth the total area. This lets the camera compensate for any variations.

DETAIL   Because the television screen is so small, all visuals should be simple and uncluttered. Too much detail, whether on an object, graph, or photograph, will be hard to see when the image is transmitted to a 19" screen. This means, for example, leaving more space between letters and lines than you would otherwise.

Figure 9.2

The use of visual aids helps to arouse and hold the attention of your audience. Imagine what this presentation would be like if the speaker tried to get you interested in geology without the map, the diagram, or the rocks.

SURFACES   Dull surfaces work better on television than glossies do. Glossy paper and shiny objects reflect light that distorts the picture.

COLOR   In black-and-white television, all colors appear as shades of gray. Most experts agree that only five or six tones of gray can be distinguished by the camera and the television screen. These are grouped below:

Black	Brown	Red	Light blue	Light gray	White
	Dark green	Medium blue	Orange	Tan	
	Dark blue	Medium green		Pastels	

When using color equipment, you must also be aware of a few potential problems. For example, color is influenced by its surroundings.

Light intensity can make something look brighter than it really should be. Colors also need to have good contrast if they are to be clear; sameness of hues will not photograph in a vivid manner.

Specific Types

Since there are more types of visuals than we can present here, we've selected five types we think you'll find most useful.

GRAPHIC MATERIAL   Most speakers call on charts, diagrams, outlines, titles, and the like when they want to seize attention, clarify a point, or prove an issue. When constructing your graphics, either on your own or with the assistance of other members of the production staff, keep the uniqueness of television foremost in your mind. That is to say, making graphics for television is not the same as making them for live presentations. Following are a few requirements for producing graphics that will look good on a small screen.

1. Keep the important details of the graphic in the center of the picture. If they're on the edges, they're apt to be left off or appear fuzzy when transmitted.

2. Select cards and posters that are a size convenient for handling, displaying, and storing. Most studios use a fourteen-ply illustration board or a dull-finish gray board. To ensure plenty of extra margin, stay within a 9 " × 12 " working area on 14" × 17 " cards, or 6 " × 8 " on 11" × 14" cards.

3. Limit outlines, lists, bar and line graphs to four or five lines. More than that will look distorted and/or run together on the screen.

4. Use dark cards and letter them with light colors, rather than using light cards with dark or black letters. This combination photographs better.

5. Make all lettering and drawing bold and clear. Printing is easier to read than exotic script.

6. Be consistent in your selection of color, design, paper, and the like. The camera will detect differences in quality, size, and texture, and such unevenness detracts from the quality of the image.

PHOTOGRAPHS   When selecting and using photographs, you should follow much the same advice we presented in our discussion of graphics. That is, be careful of too much detail, observe the rules of margin and ratio, mount the photographs on fourteen-ply gray cardboard, and remember that glossy photographs will reflect studio lights.

SLIDES AND FILMS   These forms involve somewhat more thought than do the other types of aids, because slides and films take special equipment and extra personnel. Of course, this does not preclude your using these two aids if you feel they'll enhance your presentation. However, we'll exclude equipment and personnel from our discussion and confine our analysis to the selection of appropriate slides and films.

   With 2″ × 2″ slides you must allow for a slight loss at sides, top, and bottom because of the difference in format. The television screen may "clip" a margin of as much as one-sixth the total area on all sides. The 3:4 size ratio applies to slides as well as pictures, so if your slides contain words, limit them to about six lines with no more than six words per line. The principles of clarity, unclutteredness, and contrast also apply.

   If you're planning to use films, you should know that most stations insist that all films be 16mm, either sound or silent. (Most 16mm film was not made for the small screen, so you may find that much of the detail is lost.) Keep in mind the special characteristics of television when selecting films: (1) the need for picture contrast; (2) one-sixth marginal loss of projected picture; (3) the value of closeup scenes to avoid too much detail.

   In selecting film, it is important to secure specific permission. Films, like books, are covered by copyright laws.

   Finally, as we noted earlier, seek help from the director and the technical crew well in advance of the actual production. It is unrealistic to say, two minutes to airtime, "Oh, by the way, can you show this short piece of film while I talk?" (The answer undoubtedly would be no.)

THREE-DIMENSIONAL OBJECTS   The list of props that can be used in television is limitless. You can show the audience just about anything you can get through the studio door. Paintings, cars, plants, books, antiques, cooking utensils, animals, and gems can all be put on camera. When using any three-dimensional object as a visual aid, you should try to follow these guidelines:

   1. Display the object in a way that will help the viewer understand its actual size. You could place a small object in the palm

of your hand, for example. The camera position will also influence how the object is perceived.

2. Make sure the lighting doesn't distort the object. Some articles, such as glass and jewelry, glare when hit by too much light.

3. Select objects that will photograph well. Again, this means being aware of issues such as contrast, color, and size.

4. Seek advice from the technical staff. In most instances, they will know more than you about how objects will photograph.

How to Use Visuals

The importance of consulting with the television crew can't be overemphasized. These early conversations will yield valuable information about equipment, artistic assistance, research facilities, and so on. The meetings will also allow the technical crew an opportunity to tell you how and when to display your pictures and films.

1. Make sure that the visuals you select relate to the subject you're discussing. We've seen people show pictures of their favorite subject even though the pictures had nothing to do with the topic being discussed. Showing your coin collection may interest you, but ask yourself "How does it relate to a speech on the stock market?"

2. Suit the visuals to the audience. While visuals that are too complex might confuse the audience, those that are too simple might insult them. Think about your audience analysis (Chapter 2) before you select your visuals. A crude line drawing of the inner ear would certainly offend a group of professional audiologists viewing a videotape on the dangers of loud music, for example.

3. When deciding on a visual, try to emphasize only one point. People often overwork visuals and try to demonstrate a number of points with one item. This normally results in very slow television.

4. Remember that the visuals must be seen—it is of little value to present a beautiful and informative painting if you stand in front of it. Standing in front of your material isn't an issue if it's in another part of the studio and being shown via another

camera. Just be sure to determine in advance whether the visual will be housed in another location or displayed by you.

5. Remember to maintain eye contact with the camera even when using visuals. It's tempting to focus on your graphic instead.

6. Number and/or sequence all your graphics, photographs, and slides so that they'll be easy to arrange when you're using them or moving them from place to place. Having to decide on the correct order during rehearsal or just before airtime can add to your nervousness.

7. Finally, when you rehearse your television presentation, make sure you practice with your visual material. The combination of being in the studio and having to present a visual could cause you some unnecessary apprehension. Becoming familiar with your visual could allay some of that anxiety.

PART
FOUR

THE
TELEVISION
STUDIO
REVIEW

The unfamiliarity of the studio, the often chaotic nature of rehearsals and production, can confuse and overwhelm the novice. We began by discussing the importance of knowing the personnel of the studio and what they do to contribute to a successful production. We looked at the producer, director, floor manager, floor crew, technical crew, and production assistants.

We also maintained that understanding the studio meant understanding the verbal, nonverbal and print languages of the television studio. Therefore, we mentioned the special words and actions of the television studio.

Because the equipment of the studio is such a crucial part of television, we spent some time examining cameras, microphones, recorders, switchers, editors, character generators, and visuals.

Graphic materials, photographs, slides and films, and three-dimensional objects are all possible television visuals. Like recorders, switchers, editors, and character generators, visuals contribute to the overall image created for television.

RESOURCES

Notes

1. Alan Wurtzel, *Television Production* (New York: McGraw-Hill, 1979), p. 478.
2. Herbert Zettl, *Television Production Handbook,* 4th ed. (Belmont, Calif.: Wadsworth, 1984), p. 505.
3. Thomas D. Burrows and Donald N. Wood, *Television Production,* 2nd ed. (Dubuque, Iowa: Wm. C. Brown, 1982), p. 270.

Recommended Readings

ALTEN, STANLEY. *Audio in Media.* Belmont, Calif.: Wadsworth, 1981.

HAWES, WILLIAM. *The Performer in Mass Media: In Media Professions and the Community.* New York: Hastings House, 1978.

HILLIARD, ROBERT L. *Writing for Television and Radio.* 4th ed. Belmont, Calif.: Wadsworth, 1984.

MALONEY, MARTIN, and PAUL MAX RUBENSTEIN. *Writing for Media.* Englewood Cliffs, N.J.: Prentice-Hall, 1980.

MILLERSON, GERALD. *Effective TV Production.* New York: Hastings House, 1976.

ORLIK, PETER B. *Broadcast Copywriting.* Boston: Allyn and Bacon, 1978.

PART FOUR

THE TELEVISION STUDIO

KEY: 0 = Item does not apply
         1 = Extremely well done
         2 = Fairly well done
         3 = Moderately well done
         4 = Poorly done; needs improvement

CHAPTER 7. Personnel, Parlance, and Procedures

A. Understood the studio (in general)	0 1 2 3 4
1. Understood the producer's role	0 1 2 3 4
2. Understood the director's role	0 1 2 3 4
3. Understood the floor manager's role	0 1 2 3 4
4. Understood the floor crew's role	0 1 2 3 4
5. Understood the technical crew's role	0 1 2 3 4
6. Understood the production assistant's role	0 1 2 3 4
B. Understood studio parlance (in general)	0 1 2 3 4
1. Use of studio verbal language	0 1 2 3 4
2. Use of studio gestures (hand signals)	0 1 2 3 4
C. Understood television scripting (in general)	0 1 2 3 4
1. Understood types of scripts	0 1 2 3 4
2. Preparing of the script	0 1 2 3 4
3. Marking of the script	0 1 2 3 4
4. Use of the script	0 1 2 3 4
D. Taking part in rehearsal (in general)	0 1 2 3 4
1. Participation in rehearsal meetings	0 1 2 3 4
2. Participation in technical rehearsal	0 1 2 3 4
3. Participation in run-through rehearsal	0 1 2 3 4
4. Participation in dress rehearsal	0 1 2 3 4

CHAPTER 8. Primary Television Hardware

A. Understood television cameras (in general)	0 1 2 3 4
1. Understood technical aspects	0 1 2 3 4
2. Understood visual aspects	0 1 2 3 4
3. Understood camera mounting	0 1 2 3 4
4. Understood camera movements	0 1 2 3 4
B. Understood television microphones (in general)	0 1 2 3 4
1. Understood the types of microphones (in general)	0 1 2 3 4
2. Use of studio microphones (in general)	0 1 2 3 4
3. Stayed within microphone range	0 1 2 3 4
4. Took sound checks	0 1 2 3 4
5. Eliminated distracting noises	0 1 2 3 4
6. Treatment of microphone	0 1 2 3 4
7. Adjustment of microphone	0 1 2 3 4
8. Use of original sound check	0 1 2 3 4
9. Correct distance from mouth	0 1 2 3 4
10. Spoke directly into microphone	0 1 2 3 4
11. Lavaliere properly attached	0 1 2 3 4

CHAPTER 9. Secondary Television Hardware

A. Understood video recorders	0	1	2	3	4
B. Understood switchers	0	1	2	3	4
C. Understood editors	0	1	2	3	4
D. Understood character generators	0	1	2	3	4
E. Understood special requirements of visuals (in general)	0	1	2	3	4
1. Use of correct size ratio	0	1	2	3	4
2. Aid simple and uncluttered	0	1	2	3	4
3. Use of correct surface	0	1	2	3	4
4. Use of correct colors	0	1	2	3	4
F. Understood types of visuals (in general)	0	1	2	3	4
1. Use of graphic material	0	1	2	3	4
2. Use of photographs	0	1	2	3	4
3. Use of slides and films	0	1	2	3	4
4. Use of three-dimensional articles	0	1	2	3	4
G. Use of visuals (in general)	0	1	2	3	4
1. Related to the topic being discussed	0	1	2	3	4
2. Suited to the audience	0	1	2	3	4
3. Seen by the viewers	0	1	2	3	4
4. Numbered and sequenced correctly	0	1	2	3	4
5. Use of eye contact	0	1	2	3	4

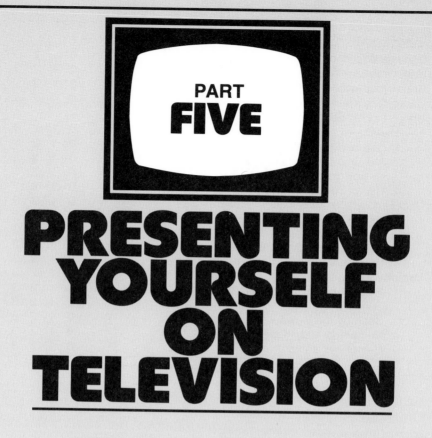

PART FIVE

PRESENTING YOURSELF ON TELEVISION

The search for effective delivery starts from a realization that vocal and physical manner are the outward form for one's beliefs, attitudes, and emotions . . . .

Donald K. Smith

We have all seen television speakers who appear to have fascinating ideas but are unable to get those ideas across with any impact. Delivery is important. People respond not only to what you say, but also to how you say it.

The acuity of the camera's eye and the sensitivity of the microphone allow little room for error. Experienced communicators understand the importance of looking and sounding their best. The purpose of this section is to explore the basic elements of sight and sound, the practical value of understanding those elements, the resources that a speaker draws on in appealing to sight and sound, and some key elements for improving television delivery. (Keep in mind that it's impossible for us to talk about all the components of communication at one time. While we may deal with them one at a time, in a full presentation they are all in operation at once.)

PART
FIVE

10. VISUAL PRESENTATION

If you're going to appear on television, you need to cultivate a sense of visual literacy. The first step is to understand the elements of sight.

In Part Four we talked about the camera and the kinds of visual aids that can be used in video presentations. In this chapter we talk about color and line as the two principal elements of television communication.

We also discuss what we call the natural human resources of visual presentation. Aside from any visual aids that you might bring to a production, most importantly you bring yourself. Posture, movement, facial expression, and eye contact are personal resources for delivering television messages effectively.

THE ELEMENTS OF SIGHT

While our explanation of sight may seem somewhat technical, keep in mind that these technical considerations can influence how viewers perceive you. Hence, those aspects of sight that we've included are the ones that you can control as you prepare for your presentation.

Color

Color is the visual element most confounding to the television novice. A suit that represents good color sense in real life may, on television, look strange and ill-fitting. To prepare for color, you should understand its basic elements: hue, saturation, and brightness.

Hue is the particular color: yellow, red, green, and so on. **Saturation** refers to the strength of color: maroon as opposed to shell pink. **Brightness** is determined by whether a color, when translated to black and white, reproduces as a light or a dark gray.

These three elements have an effect on flesh color, background, and clothes. For example, the dominant flesh hue is red. Most backdrops are blue, because blue clarifies red. If a red backdrop were used, your skin tone would tend to merge with it—an interesting effect, but not an attractive one.

MAKEUP Skin hue lacks saturation, which is why skin looks washed out on television. Makeup is almost invariably used to enhance the video image. The only way to determine how much and what kind of makeup you need is to do a video test. Seek some help in determining the results of that test. Over two hundred years ago, Voltaire noted, "It is not love we should have painted blind, but self-love." Indeed, we are often poor judges of how we look.

You can choose between oil-base and powdered makeup. If you're familiar with makeup, then your task is primarily a matter of working with your skin hues until they come out the way you want them in a test. If you have no experience in this area, find someone who does, or purchase a makeup kit and experiment.

Keep in mind that makeup must be balanced and withstand close scrutiny. Oil-based mixtures will shine under the studio lights unless screened with a powder. If your makeup is too exaggerated, a closeup can make you look like a clown.

As a general rule, makeup shouldn't include much blue or red. The safest course is to stick to oranges, browns, and tans. Also remember that some viewers may be watching on black-and-white sets, and makeup should be applied accordingly. For example, dark blue–red lipstick may come out as a dark gray or black line on black-and-white television.

The rules for makeup are based on common sense. Flesh is basically red; a blue backdrop complements red. Orange, brown, and tan hues balance and complement red and blue. A bald person may need his head "touched-up" a little, and a black or darkly-tanned speaker will not have the same makeup demands as a pale Caucasian.

CLOTHES   Just as skin hue might disappear into a red background, so might a blue suit get lost in a blue background. In most situations, it's best to stay away from reds and blues. As a general rule, pink, green, tan, and gray all reproduce well on both color and black-and-white television.

Saturation is a significant variable in television dress. Intense colors form solid blocks in black-and-white reproduction; if you use solid colors, you must keep in mind that balance is important. A green and blue of the same saturation may reproduce to the same gray; what may seem balanced in color may, in black and white, be a travesty. Dull saturation is best for television—tan rather than yellow. Again, experimentation is a good practice.

Brightness, too, must be taken into consideration when choosing your television wardrobe. As with saturation, colors that have the same degree of brightness may, on a black-and-white receiver, reproduce to the same gray.

When you wear or present a bright object in front of the camera, it has extra weight in the composition, which should be balanced with another bright area or with a larger mass of dull saturation. Remember that the eye is drawn to the bright and the colorful. If you wear chartreuse socks, your ankles might become the viewer's focal point. In general, color sense in television is similar to what it is in the rest of your life: a matter of practical consideration and observation.

One color effect that surprises many novices to television speaking is the **moiré effect**—narrow or contrasting color stripes that produce vibrations on the screen. Stay away from these kinds of stripes.

White and black are visual elements in color television and should also be considered by anyone preparing to appear on camera. White is not a good clothes choice. First, it reflects other colors; if you dress in white, you're liable to find yourself reflecting every skin, set, and studio color. Second, if you wear white, there is a tendency for the other colors around you to go dark. Third, if you are in a white environment, you and your coloring tend to go dark. These problems *can* be solved with lighting, set changes, and makeup, but it's questionable whether white clothing is worth the extra effort.

Black tends to pale skin hue and, like other dark shades, tends to move toward the background. Black-and-white combinations, like color combinations, should be thought about before use.

There are exceptions to every piece of advice. For example, black and white should not be avoided if you're working with black-and-white videotape. Black-and-white television, like black-and-white photography, is worth pursuing from the standpoint of composition and contrast. Black and white may enhance a documentary effect, establish a mood, and, as in the movie *The Wizard of Oz,* can be used as a prelude and contrast to color.

Just as there are reasons for not avoiding black and white, so there are reasons that might lead a television speaker to wear blue, bright, or narrow-striped clothes. The rules we mention in this book are general rules—specific situations and needs may require experimentation and research.

Line

Line is important to television speakers in terms of dress and stance. It can make the difference between success and failure.

Horizontal lines in clothes will add the impression of weight. It has been suggested that television adds about ten pounds to your appearance. So if you're of average weight, television will make you look slightly chunky, even without horizontal stripes. Vertical lines, on the other hand, will impart an image of thinness. You can consciously alter your appearance, therefore, by choosing horizontal or vertical lines in your clothes.

But the general advice of professionals is to avoid stripes altogether. If the stripes are colored, they can lead to the moiré effect. If the set includes similar stripes, you may blend into the background. If the background contains striping opposite to that in the clothes, the effect may be "busy."

Line is also a factor in your stance. If you're standing in an awkward position, your shoulders and head may reflect that awkwardness and you may seem out of balance to your viewers. Maintaining good posture, keeping your body on an even keel, is particularly significant in television because the head and upper torso are often the visual focus. We'll talk more about posture later in this chapter.

Posture is not the only aspect of stance where line matters. You should also be aware of line of sight as an indicator of stance. You can stand even with, higher than, or lower than the camera. Each of these stances is perceived differently by the audience. Line of sight can establish an attitude as well as physical position in television presentations. Line, like color, is a visual concern of television speakers.

YOUR PHYSICAL BEARING

As you would suspect, effective use of the visual aspect of television involves much more than knowing about color and line. Your total visual impression is directly related to your natural physical resources. In considering television delivery, it is critical to examine the visual appeals of posture, movement, facial expression, and eye contact.

Posture

In talk shows there are three common postures. You can sit on the couch in a stiff, ramrod position; you can slouch as if having trouble staying awake; you can sit relaxed, shoulders back, and still be comfortable. The rigid posture conveys tension, anxiety, nervousness. The slouchy posture conjures up an image of apathy, boredom, and torpor. The third posture suggests vigor and comfort. Posture tends to be contagious; if you appear comfortable and at ease, the other members on the panel, and even those watching, feel more relaxed.

Keep the following few rules in mind as you think about posture.

1. Be natural. Beginners often find it difficult to carry out this seemingly easy bit of advice. Not only are they nervous, but most first-timers also tend to copy someone they've seen on television—usually a professional whose style is unique. Try as they might, these newcomers can't sit in the same relaxed manner as Burt Reynolds or move with the same flair as Joan Rivers, and the attempts are embarrassing to watch. Be yourself.

2. Remember that your posture must be compatible with your message. A formal stand-up speech on a serious topic will call for a slightly different posture than will the telling of a joke.

3. Try to adapt your posture to the constraints imposed by the studio or setting. How far you sit from other people, social conventions, number of people on the set, and props (or the lack of them) will all influence your posture.

4. Be prepared to change posture quickly should the need arise. Camera movements, microphone placement, and signals from your director may force you to shift positions on very short notice. You may have to move from giving a speech to being a member of a panel discussion. The first is likely to be formal, the latter informal. In addition, the equipment you use in the studio will demand that you adapt to or make changes in the environment. For example, a microphone on the table shouldn't force you to lean forward in an awkward position; an overhead boom shouldn't make you look up.

5. Be careful with chairs. Most interview programs, for example, use swivel chairs as part of their set. Swaying back and forth in your chair like an impatient child while discussing your company's operations in unfriendly countries diminishes your credibility.

Movement

The camera, as we've noted throughout, can create the illusion of movement. It can move back and forth, up and down. With the zoom lens it can make you appear close even when it's some distance away. This means that there may be many shots that you've not even aware of, shots that affect the movement and distance between you and the people watching their sets.

Even though much of the movement the viewer sees may be beyond your immediate control, you can influence the overall visual effect of your presentation in the following ways:

1. While most shots of you will focus on your head and shoulders, you must be aware that the rest of your body will become tense if you try to keep from moving. The restraint of your gestures, or lack of them, will show up on the screen; if not through your body, through your voice. Therefore, be yourself, be natural, and allow yourself some movement. This means striking a balance between frozen immobility and aimless pacing and gesturing.

2. Although we just urged you to be natural, television does impose some limitations on your movement.

   a. Avoid sweeping and rapid gestures. Such movements are often difficult for the camera operator to follow. Learn to gesture a little more slowly than normal when you appear on television.

   b. Don't gesture directly toward the camera—it can cause considerable distortion.

   c. Don't cross your legs quickly—it's often visually awkward.

3. When you're in a closeup shot, you should keep your gestures close to your body. If they become too large, they'll be out of the picture frame. Think how silly you'll look if the viewers see your arms and wrists but not your hands.

4. If you're asked to stand in one exact spot that is designated in tape or chalk, allow some movement of your shoulders, arms, or

Figure 10.1

It's important to be yourself on television. The passion evident in this man's demeanor encourages audience interest.

hands. Simply shifting from leg to leg, swaying, or leaning will make you look nervous, awkward, as though you're about to tip over.

5. Make sure that your gestures are appropriate to the topic and occasion. Gesticulating vigorously when talking on a somber subject might be interpreted as a sign of insincerity; large gestures are out of place when you're sitting on a couch during a one-to-one interview.

6. Try to control any idiosyncratic mannerisms that are apt to call attention to themselves. All of us have nervous habits, such as tapping our fingers on a table or fiddling with our eyeglasses. These tics are magnified by the keen eye of the camera. Become aware of your personal distracting movements and keep them in check.

7. When walking, move with ease. Keeping your weight on the balls of your feet will help. In addition, take small, slow steps so that the camera will be able to follow you.

8. If you plan to use props, graphs, and charts, or do a great deal
of moving, you should practice these movements before the actual program. The director will be glad to work them out with
you during rehearsal. In this way your movements will not confuse the camera operator. If you're moving right when the camera is going left, embarrassment results.

Facial Expressions

Given our emphasis on naturalness, it seems contradictory to discuss facial expressions. Yet the camera calls attention to the simplest of facial
subtleties. A wide range of emotions and attitudes are conveyed by your
face, and your audience will attach meaning to these expressions
whether you want them to or not. While we urge you to be yourself, you
must also be mindful of the message you are sending. Being deadpan,
for example, would most likely be perceived as being dull and uninteresting; smiling while describing a hotel fire would certainly impair
your credibility.

One final note regarding facial expressions: Since you can never
know for certain when a closeup shot is being broadcast, you should act
as if the camera were on your face at all times. This means that you
should be concerned with how you look for as long as the red tally light
is on, even if the camera isn't pointed directly at you. We have seen
many first-time performers look foolish because they thought the camera was focused elsewhere.

Eye Contact

This is perhaps the one aspect of television delivery that causes the
greatest amount of personal apprehension. The untrained performer is
not only nervous (which, of course, influences eye contact), but seldom
knows where to look and for how long. In normal face-to-face interaction, the rules and uses of eye contact are learned early as part of our
culture. Each of us knows that we use our eyes to indicate when we
want to talk to the person in front of us and when we want to avoid
communication. We can even indicate who we like and dislike by our
gaze. But what happens when we can't see the person we're talking to—
and they can see us? What set of rules do we use?

The National Association of Broadcasters offers some excellent advice: "Remember that although you are talking to a large audience, you
should pretend you are speaking to a few friends who are in their
homes."[1] This can be translated into some practical recommendations:

1. Look directly at the camera that is "on" (the one with the red light). And look at the activated camera about 100 percent of the time that you're talking. Breaking your gaze, at least on television, gives the impression that you've lost your place or are being shifty. If the red tally light changes, or if the floor manager points to another camera, simply transfer your eyes to the other camera as smoothly as possible. With practice, these transitions will become graceful. For now, the important thing to remember is to try to imagine that the person you're talking to is inside the camera.

2. Try not to yield to all the distractions that will encourage your eyes to leave the camera. Many television speakers, even some professionals, have a hard time resisting the temptation to look at themselves on the studio monitors.

   Another common distraction is the normal activity of any production. It's difficult to not look away from the camera as the camera operator crawls away on hands and knees to make some repairs or adjustments in the set. But a break in eye contact can be perceived as deception or some form of uneasiness. Therefore, ignore these extraneous events. Let the other members of the crew worry about production: Concentrate on your audience and your presentation.

3. Knowing the target of your message will also influence your use of eye contact. That is to say, although the "on" camera is normally the place for you to focus your gaze, there are some occasions when your eye contact will be elsewhere. For example, when you're being interviewed, you should look directly at the interviewer. The same is true when you're on a panel or in a small group. You are to interact with, which means look at, the people with you. The people watching their sets are simply sharing the transaction. On the rare occasions when you wish to direct something to the viewing audience, you should locate the camera with the red light and speak to it.

4. Don't stare at the camera as if you've been hypnotized. We've seen countless performers become transfixed by the camera; they gape unblinkingly at it. You wouldn't do this in face-to-face conversation, and you shouldn't do it on television. Treat the camera as a person.

5. If a "live" audience is present, look at them, not at the camera. However, make sure the television audience knows that there's a studio audience.

A great fear of all beginners is that they'll forget what they want to say, be it a few lines or an entire formal speech. Each performer must, of course, discover the memory aid that he or she feels most comfortable with.

If you're fortunate enough to be using a studio that has a Tele-PrompTer, you should take time to learn how to use it. This device can take a variety of mechnical forms. Basically it is a screen mounted on the camera, just above the lens, that can carry your entire presentation or just a few notes. The copy moves as you talk. The location of the Tele-PrompTer makes it relatively easy for you to look at it as you're looking into the camera. Some models even have your words or cues appearing in the lens, so you don't have to look up or down.

Figure 10.2

"Idiot cards" are often used when TelePrompTers are unavailable or inaccessible. Here an assistant reads along with the speaker so that she can flip the cards at an appropriate time without causing the speaker to stumble over words. Note that the cards are positioned directly under the camera, so that it will appear that the speaker is talking directly to the television audience. Photography by Scott Highton. Courtesy of Power/Rector Productions.

   The TelePrompTer, like all memory aids, is not free from risks. It can make you look silly and unprofessional, as your eyes flick left to right, left to right.

   Using a TelePrompTer in a mechanical, unthinking way can lead to trouble. For example, a local news announcer recently had to shift from an upbeat, fun-at-the-beach, human-interest story to a story about a train wreck. He unwittingly continued the pace he had established with the first story, light and fast, into the second story; the result was that the newscaster appeared silly, if not insensitive. If you're going to use a TelePrompTer, rehearse with it so that you can establish appropriate tempos for your material.

   You can also put some notes on large poster boards and ask a member of the studio crew to hold them and change them as you move through your presentation. If you use this method, make sure you practice, number your posters, and use large, clear lettering so that you can

Figure 10.3

Notes can be useful in interviews. This woman is not at all afraid to consult her notes while on camera. Such a practice can indicate a concern for getting the facts right, promoting the audience's confidence in your objectivity (if you're the host) or accuracy (if you're the guest). Referring to notes too often, however, may give the impression that you don't know your subject well.

look at the camera as much as possible. One sure way to distinguish a television novice from an expert is in the use of off-camera aids. The novice looks only at the aid, while the professional looks at the aid while also looking at the camera.

Finally, there might be instances when you want to have your notes on camera with you. There's nothing wrong with notes. But don't try to conceal the fact that you're using them. Many professional interviewers, such as Johnny Carson and David Frost, let their viewers know they're using memory aids. Some people even believe that using a clipboard or notes can enhance their image of professionalism. The danger of using notes is that they often become a reason for looking away from either the camera or the person you're talking to. Frantically searching for something you wrote down instead of looking at the camera can tarnish your credibility and lose the audience. When using notecards or any carry-on memory aid, remember these few simple rules:

1. Become familiar with the content of the cards.

2. Refer to them only as you need them.

3. Make sure they are easy to read.

4. Don't let them keep you from looking at your in-person or video audience.

5. Make sure your notes are numbered and in the proper sequence before beginning.

SUMMARY

Posture, movements, facial expression and eye contact are visual appeals to sight. How we handle our hands, our face, and our eyes often determines the outcome of our television as much as our face-to-face interactions.

The basic visual elements of color, line, and motion, as well as posture and movement, are not the only visual concerns in using television. The camera, the visuals, the lighting, and numerous other factors contribute to making your television message visually exciting.

A television speaker may not control all the visual factors of a given television presentation, but understanding the various visual elements lends a speaker the ability to exert some visual control in his or her presentation.

11. SOUND PRESENTATION

The word *television* can lead one to suppose that *vision* is dominant in this medium. But to overlook the equally important role of sound would be a serious mistake. We are here reminded of the quotation from *The Spectator:* "I have often lamented that we cannot close our ears with as much ease as we can our eyes."[2] For a long time people have realized that "the voice is a second face." The ancient Greeks recognized its importance. Before the advent of writing, they chanted and sang their poems and stories. After writing developed, one of their greatest scholars, Aristotle, defined speech delivery in much the same way as we might describe song, as "essentially a matter of the right management of the voice to express the various emotions."[3]

Volume, articulation, rate, and pitch have evolved as the primary elements in "the right management of the voice" for television communication. Not only can these elements be controlled by the speaker, they can be manipulated electronically. The second task of this chapter is to discuss the place of microphones in delivering your television message.

THE VARIABLES OF SOUND

Volume

Volume has meaning in human communication: When we listen, we make decisions on the basis of volume, and in speaking we manipulate volume to convey meaning and direction to the decisions being made. The first requisite of vocal sound is that we employ enough volume to be heard. On television, this task is often simplified by the fact that volume can be increased and/or decreased by the sound engineer. Even if you're using a small home unit to record your presentation, you can have a friend control the volume while you're speaking. Decide what is a comfortable and natural volume and aim for that level.

Once you've identified your comfort level, there are a few additional considerations that could aid you in your efforts. While attaining a comfortable volume, you should also think about how you can employ changes in your loudness level as a means of getting and sustaining attention. You know from your own experience that a voice that stays at the same level is seldom interesting to listen to. Uttering a word at an intensity level different from that used with the other words in a sentence can direct attention to that word. Some research suggests that a sudden change to a softer level is likely to be more effective than the opposite. This, of course, is contrary to the common belief that you have to yell to get attention. Raising your voice may call attention to yourself, but it seldom helps emphasize your words.

When analyzing your use of volume on television, try to avoid an error made by many novices. During rehearsal, the audio engineer asks you to say something so that the controls can be set. You mumble into the mike, or count to three in a low, subdued voice. The engineer adjusts the volume being transmitted. Then, when the show starts, you boom out your opening lines. Remember, your control over volume begins with the first microphone test. Establish a normal volume in the first test and maintain that approximate volume throughout the presentation.

One final note concerning volume on television: If you're not in a studio, you may have to speak in a louder-than-normal voice. For example, loud ambient noise—traffic, a convention, a factory—may compete with your voice level. Being prepared for these situations and making the necessary adjustments is one of the signs of a pro.

Articulation

Articulation is the clarity of expression. If you mumble your words, and if you mispronounce your words, then you're apt to be misunderstood. In addition, our culture expects educated people to speak in a clear and proper manner, and a violation of this cultural norm can lower your credibility. Ask yourself how often you are persuaded or informed by a someone who leaves the *g* off *ing* endings or says *git* for *get*.

Unlike volume, articulation is the sole responsibility of the speaker. The best electronic equipment made will not straighten out a mumbled sentence—it will only transmit it. Sloppy speech sounds even sloppier when broadcast. (There are exceptions to every rule. Comedians, for example, sometimes mumble and mispronounce words as a means of getting a laugh. But most people on TV need to be serious about articulation.)

One of the first steps in solving articulation problems is becoming aware of what these problems are, and the forms they are likely to take. A comprehensive listing would be a major undertaking, for in one sense there are as many problems as there are speakers. However, most errors in articulation fall within the following broad categories.

1. Simple laziness often causes poor enunciation. Consonants such as *p, b, v,* and *f* are the most common victims of this lazy attitude. Notice how poor articulation is evident if you misplace your tongue when producing consonants like *t, d, k,* and *g.* The same can be said for vowel sounds. But when striving for precision, avoid overpreciseness, which is often perceived as a sign of affectation and insincerity.

2. Trying to use a dialect that isn't your own can cause articulation problems. In the continental United States there are four general dialects: Southern, Eastern, Midwestern, and General American. While the latter is the ideal in most mass communications, you need not try to emulate the news staff of CBS if you normally speak in the Southern or Eastern dialect. In short, be correct in your speech, but also be yourself; the words will come more easily.

3. Not knowing the correct pronunciation of foreign place names, proper names, and difficult words can lead novices to slur their words as they try to fake their way through. The press services and the networks compile lists of foreign and difficult words, providing phonetic pronunciation guides. If you have doubts about any word, consult a good contemporary pronouncing dictionary. This type of book can even help you with simple but troublesome words such as *penalize, athletics, address, status, adult,* and *data.* The pronunciation of names like Khomeini and words like *junta* may also be learned by listening to news announcers.

4. Sound substitutions and omissions can hinder comprehension. Notice the confusion and potential misunderstandings that can occur if you aren't careful when you articulate some of the following words: "slep" for *slept,* "goin" for *going,* "sinator" for *senator,* "jist" for *just,* "cuz" for *because,* "Illinoise" for *Illinois,* "zackly" for *exactly,* and so on.

5. Tension can cause articulation problems. Try to relax your throat so that the muscles needed for articulation can work freely. Make sure you have an ample supply of air so that you won't need to cut your words off before they're finished. And strive for strong and active movements of your lips, tongue, and jaw.

As we said, any list of possible errors is bound to be incomplete. Each person has a natural, personal voice, but the odds are pretty good that everyone also has some flaw in vocal delivery. Only close observation and rigorous practice will reveal and correct the problem, whatever it may be. Listening to the radio and television can help you find vocal models. Reading and candid assessments by others can contribute to the understanding and control of sound delivery. We also suggest that you buy a small tape recorder—and use it!

Rate

People's rate of delivery ranges from around 100 to 150 words per minute. The average is somewhere around 130 to 170 wpm. The top speed for a listener's comprehension is 285 wpm, though some would argue that it is as high as 500. Television speech averages about 162 wpm; news announcers may sometimes get up to 190.

People new to broadcasting tend, erroneously, to speak slowly. This practice is as absurd as the tendency to speak slowly to someone who doesn't understand English well. In television, time is expensive, and those using the medium generally try to get the most for their money. If anything, you should step up your speaking rate on television. Listen to yourself and contrast what you hear with the rate of speaking in programs similar to yours. Do you sound draggy and slow? If so, pick up your rate; give it some life and vitality.

That television is a medium of fast audio was particularly apparent in the situation comedy *Mork and Mindy.* According to researcher Pat Dowling, Mork (Robin Williams) spoke at a rate surpassing 200 words per minute. As we noted above, the average rate on television is 162 wpm.[4]

Talking faster is not the only way rate is used on television. Just as volume needs to be varied to hold attention, so does rate. Talk faster, then slower, then fast again, pause, speed up, and soon, you'll find that you'll be easier to listen to.

Pitch

Pitch, though often difficult to control, represents another tool at the disposal of the television speaker. A pitch that's too high is usually quite piercing when magnified by the microphone. Yet being nervous, as many people are when appearing on television, is the number one cause of a high and unpleasant pitch. Therefore, we urge you once again to try to relax your entire body, and particularly your throat, when speaking on television.

Although we just stressed the importance of trying to avoid a high-pitched voice, we should also add that changes in pitch (raising pitch at the end of a sentence instead of lowering it), at least within your normal range, can be an effective means of gaining attention and imparting meaning. In short, varying your pitch is yet another way you can avoid a monotone as you speak on television.

USING MICROPHONES

When you speak in front of a camera, you're also speaking in front of a microphone. We discussed the technical aspects of microphones in Chapter 8; the following tips tell you how to work with the microphone to help your presentation.

1. Remember to stay within microphone range so that your voice can be broadcast to your audience. The correct range will usually be determined by the audio engineer. Your job is to make sure you don't walk away from or turn away from the microphone unless you know for certain you can be heard. This means knowing the range of the boom and/or how much cord you have left on your lavaliere. (If you run out of cord, don't jerk—you'll unplug the entire unit.)

2. Don't alter your pitch or volume range too much from the original volume check. Distortion may occur if you increase or decrease your volume, pitch, or rate without the control room knowing about it, although a good sound technician can usually compensate for such variations.

3. Don't put the microphone too close to your mouth. A good distance for a hand-held microphone is approximately one foot below and slightly in front of the mouth. This enables the camera to photograph your face. It also improves the quality of sound.

4. Don't speak directly into the microphone. Try to visualize yourself speaking across it instead of into it. This will give your voice a more natural sound.

5. Be careful with *s, ch,* and *sh* sounds. The microphone exaggerates these sibilant (hissing) sounds. Spend some time learning to "swallow" these sounds and concentrating on the sound that precedes or follows them. For example, focus on *ga* in *gas,* and *ould* in *should.* You might also be wary of *p, v, t,* and *b* sounds. If they are stressed, they create a "popping" sound. Asthmatic or heavy breathing is also magnified by the microphone, so be careful not to breathe directly into it.

6. Remember that a microphone is a highly sensitive instrument, engineered to pick up *all* sound, not just your voice. Therefore, avoid wearing clothing and accessories that make noise. The rattling of your jewelry can sound like a full orchestra if it's sent over the airwaves. You should also refrain from moving paper too near the microphone. Tapping the microphone is also on the list of taboos.

CONTROLLING NERVOUSNESS

Television, as we have noted elsewhere, can be an overwhelming experience. Even accomplished speakers may feel a touch of fear as they find themselves face-to-face with a camera. All of us can have a presentation ruined by stage fright and unnecessary apprehension. Anyone using television would do well to understand why such fright exists and what can be done about it.

Understanding Stage Fright

The best way to understand stage fright is to begin with two interrelated premises. First, stage fright is quite natural, and second, nearly everyone suffers from it. You are not an anomaly just because adrenalin rushes into your bloodstream and makes your heart race. The wet hands and goosepimples are also not unique to you. Like other people, professionals and amateurs, you fear looking silly in front of other people, and hence are bound to feel some nervousness. But unlike the professional broadcaster, you're apt to feel some anxiety because television is a new

Figure 11.1

Arrive early, inspect the surroundings, and —if you have time—relax with the other participants before the show. Feeling comfortable in your environment and with your fellow presenters inevitably leads to a smoother presentation.

medium for you. Both of these are reasonable fears, but they *can* be vanquished.

Overcoming Stage Fright

Controlling the fears you may have about appearing on television involves three steps. You can cope with anxieties before the presentation; there are techniques you can employ during your presentation that will reduce anxiety; finally, experienced television speakers generally find that it is also necessary to alleviate the stresses of television presentation after the presentation is finished. It's not healthy to maintain a continued state of anxiety; easing the pressure in stages helps.

BEFORE THE PERFORMANCE   You can begin coping with stage fright by spending some time seriously thinking about whom you will be talking to. Reducing uncertainty about your audience can eliminate much of the worry associated with television presentation.

You can also help control nervousness before the program starts by inspecting the physical environment (studio, auditorium, office, etc.) before you actually go on camera. By knowing in advance the peculiarities of the setting, and the limitations they might impose, you can make the necessary adjustments and also not be disarmed by the activity that is often part of a television production.

As the time for your appearance grows closer, start practicing these tension-reducing techniques.

1. Engage in excessive yawning just before you go on camera. As silly as it sounds, and as funny as you may think you look (and you will), exaggerated yawning gives you extra oxygen while also relaxing your throat muscles.

2. Stretch. Stretching relaxes your muscles and also occupies your attention just before the floor manager signals you onto the set.

3. If possible, try to take a small drink of water as part of your pre-program preparation. This will help reduce the "cottonmouth" feeling that tension often produces.

4. Develop a good mental attitude—*want* to appear on television. This last suggestion is often easier said than done. But looking forward to the experience can help you overcome feelings of apprehension.

DURING THE PERFORMANCE   Anxiety during a television presentation can be handled in two ways, depending on whether the presentation is live or pretaped. On live television, the luxury of an error is not yours to enjoy. If you're broadcasting live, and anxiety leads you to an error, you have the same choices you have in life. You can admit the error ("I misspoke myself; what I mean is . . .") and proceed onward in the hope that you don't end up with both feet in your mouth before it's all over. Or you can pretend that the error didn't happen and hope that your audience is a forgiving one.

Job interviewing and group conferencing represent television situations that generally demand live television. Most other television presentations are pretaped and edited.

If you make a mistake in pretaped television, you can simply stop and try again. Pretaped material can also be divided, added to, subtracted from, and thoroughly edited. If you have editing facilities at your command, then you have no worries during a presentation.

Most television crews take breaks of one sort or another, during which you can compose yourself. In situations where there are no breaks, it's advisable to have a drink of water; a drink not only takes care of the parched feeling produced by television lights and television anxiety, it gives you a moment's respite. Just remember that your glass or cup is a small and fragile liferaft and will not carry you too far or too often.

AFTER THE PERFORMANCE   If you're prepared for your presentation, you'll find yourself increasingly comfortable as you proceed. If your anxiety continues unabated throughout your presentation, then you'll probably have to make an effort to calm yourself when it's over. Technical editing can't exorcise the anxieties a television speaker may have after a presentation.

Professionals admit that working in television is exhausting. It takes a lot of energy to deal with the equipment and people that make television presentations possible. After a lengthy presentation, most people involved are either "hyper" or depressed. Television tension lingers on after the production is finished.

Watching a tape of your performance would seem to be counterproductive—you'd be reliving rather than relieving your anxiety. However, if you sit and watch those reruns long enough, you'll find you reach some level of objectivity and relaxation. In studying your presentation, you see not only what you did wrong, but what you did right. You also begin to see how you could do better.

Once you have granted and accepted the premise that being apprehensive is normal, you can develop specific strategies for managing this apprehension. One of the best things you can do is reflected in the adage that "Practice makes perfect." The more you appear on television, the easier it will become. You should, therefore, look for opportunities that will place you on the television. The sheer repetition and exposure will help you overcome your fear and your nervousness.

IMPROVING TELEVISION DELIVERY

Most people come to the television experience with all the abilities they need to send other people messages: talking, walking, gesturing, and the like. How you use those abilities helps determine your effectiveness.

In this chapter we have offered advice about the aural elements of television presentation. However, we wonder if calling special attention to the natural resources of communication hasn't created a situation similar to that depicted in the novel *Confessions of Zeno* by Italo Svevo. The title character is told by a friend that each human step takes a half a second and involves at least fifty-four muscles. Zeno thinks about his next step and finds "something terrifically complicated which seemed to get out of order directly I began thinking about it." The attempt at control left Zeno impaired and "for several days afterwards walking became a burden."[5] The act of delivering our television messages is no less complex than walking; too much focus on delivery may impair delivery.

As so many authorities have noted, delivery is a natural thing and should simply follow the forms of human address. While we agree in part with this position, we also believe that nature alone is not always enough. There are times when some assistance is needed. So, while admitting that we run the risk of making you overly self-conscious like Zeno, we shall in this last section continue to analyze the complexities of delivery.

Improving your delivery on television does not begin and end with just one appearance or with the reading of a single chapter. If you want to be truly effective in the use of television you must adopt a long-range training program—a program that should include practice, review, seeking advice, locating and developing models, and experimenting.

Practice

In the early days of television, equipment was scarce. Practice with the medium was uncommon, and many people won and lost a spot in the lineup in a matter of a few attempts. The quantity of equipment and outlets for television speaking has so increased that practice is possible for anyone wanting it.

Television delivery is best practiced with at least three people: one on the camera, one in front of the camera, and one on the recorder. Sometimes the three people might specialize in their various tasks; sometimes it's valuable to trade spots so that everyone has a chance to experience a fuller range of television production.

Review

Practice isn't much help without review. Video recordings, like sound recordings, are always surprising to novices—the camera and recorder function as eye and ear, and often what they see and hear is not what we think we look or sound like. Review of television practice can reveal limitations in equipment and scenery as well as in the performer's delivery.

Beyond the striking first impressions you may glean in reviewing your tape, there are numerous, more subtle subsequent impressions. In our teaching, we try to rerun a practice shot as often as our students wish. With few exceptions, most of them find enough to think about in one or two reviews.

Generally, after two or three practices of a particular presentation, our students begin to look and sound fairly good; that is, they work their way to better presentations on their own. Sometimes, however, a problem remains; something is not as it should be, and lack of experience makes it difficult for the novice speaker to either pinpoint or correct the problem.

Practice and review are seldom productive if they are random or lack focus. Part of productive focus is knowing what to look for while you're reviewing the tapes of your presentation. If your concern is with delivery, you might concentrate on some of the following questions.

Did you have enough vocal variety to hold attention?

Was your eye contact focused in the right direction?

Did your wardrobe and accessories videotape to your advantage?

Did your voice add to or detract from the presentation?

Did you engage in any distracting mannerisms?

Did you need makeup? Was the makeup correctly applied?

Did you talk too fast or slow?

Did you look interested in what you were talking about?

Did your posture communicate a positive impression?

Did you appear nervous?

Was your walking, gesturing, and so on, natural?

Did you enunciate clearly?

What was the overall impression given to the viewer?

Many of these questions can be answered if you can afford to buy, or can gain access to, a small video recorder and learn how to use it.

Seeking Advice

Beyond practice and review, good advice is helpful to include as part of your training program. But sometimes securing good advice is a difficult task: How do you decide whom you should listen to? Let's begin our answer by telling you who *not* to listen to. People who have appeared on television ten or fifteen times—but have never been good at it (although they don't know it)—may have lots of advice and many stories, but don't be fooled into thinking they are experts. Be careful of the person who equates quality with quantity. Seek out people you have seen and admired on television. You have enough good sense to know if someone is a successful communicator. These are the people to advise you.

Be selective when you ask for advice and when it is given to you unsolicited. Don't be timid; ask specific questions whenever you can.

You must decide when in the evolution of your presentation you want others to offer their recommendations. Needless to say, advice given before you appear on television ("Don't wear too much makeup") is going to be different from that given after you are seen ("You talked much too slow"). Often it's helpful to make a practice tape of yourself and have people who have been successful on television evaluate it for you.

In trying to locate people to help you, look for those who are not only knowledgeable but who are also honest and candid. Having a group of your friends tell you that you should have your own network talk show is not a learning experience.

When you do find qualified people who are willing to share their observations with you, it can be a rewarding encounter. Experience is learning from failures and successes. It is making errors, but soon turning them into profit. Therefore, seeking someone with experience who is willing to lend a helping eye and ear is a worthwhile endeavor for anyone just beginning to learn the television language.

Locating and Developing Models

In ancient Rome, students had to memorize great speeches and deliver them as they were said to have been delivered originally. Mimicry is not great speaking, but it can reveal some of the powerful elements of communication that have moved, taught, and touched great numbers of people. The principle behind imitating others is that there is an essence of good speaking, an essence that can be captured by closely associating with its previous manifestations.

We think there are some standard ingredients of good communication. We also believe that most of us know good communication when we see and hear it. Consequently, pinpointing those people we consider good communicators and attempting to do what they do can provide valuable lessons.

We've watched Clarke, Cooke, and Child and seen them as models of educational television. What Clarke does for art, what Cooke does for literature, and what Child does for food illustrates how appreciation courses can be conveyed via the medium of television.

As the plurality of our preferences suggests, we think it wise to select more than one model. If you pattern yourself on only one person, you risk becoming a carbon copy. In watching television production classes and local news programs, we've noticed that there are a number of ersatz Dan Rathers around. When we advocate finding models, we're not talking about the cloning of television personalities.

There are, then, two kinds of models that we draw on to improve television delivery. The first model is based on what *is;* the best of reality. The second model is based on what *could* or *should be;* the best of our dreams and ideals. Both models are helpful in television production since both represent a standard by which we can judge our efforts.

Experimentation

In the thirty-some years that commercial television has been in existence, standard models of delivery have evolved. Sometimes those models may not suit your needs, or they may strike you as outdated. In such cases we recommend experimentation—taking the initiative and trying out new and different forms of delivery.

We have learned some good things from our attempts at experimentation. We have tried varying our speaking rate, posture, eye contact, and the like, depending on the type and the content of the program. Even experimenting with different wardrobes taught us something about our image and how we came across.

PART FIVE

PRESENTING YOURSELF ON TELEVISION

REVIEW

Sight and sound are the primary components of television delivery. They are the means of making contact with the audience. In examining sight and sound in television communications, we have noted the various elements of each and then suggested how those elements affect the person standing in front of the camera.

The basic assumption of this section has been that communicating successfully on television demands that you adapt and adjust the skills of delivery to the medium. Part of that adaptation means learning about how you are seen and heard. The first steps of understanding sight are knowing the role of color, line, and motion. These three components of vision will influence such things as the clothes you wear, your use of makeup, your selection of jewelry and accessories, and the like. Being seen on television also demands that you be aware of your posture, movement, facial expressions, and eye contact.

Sound is also part of your television presentation. You must learn to control your volume, articulation, rate, and pitch.

Because we believe that improvement should be part of any training program we suggested that you practice, review, seek advice, locate and develop models, and experiment.

RESOURCES

Notes

1. "So You're Going on TV," National Association of Broadcasters (Washington, D.C., 1978).
2. Richard Steele, *The Spectator,* as quoted in *The International Thesaurus of Quotations* (New York: Thomas Y. Crowell, Publishers, 1970), p. 627.
3. Aristotle, *Rhetoric,* Rhys Roberts, trans. (New York: Random House, 1954), p. 164.
4. Patrick S. Dowling, *Speed: A Variable Component in the Commercial Television Communication Process,* master's thesis at the University of Nevada, Las Vegas, 1979.
5. Italo Svevo, *Confessions of Zeno* (New York: Vintage Books, 1958), pp. 94–95.

Recommended Readings

SOUND

ALTEN, STANLEY R. *Audio in Media.* Belmont, Calif.: Wadsworth, 1981.

CRINGEL, ROBERT. *Audio Control Handbook.* 5th ed. New York: Hastings House, 1984.

RIZZO, RAYMOND. *The Voice as an Instrument.* New York: Odyssey Press, 1969.

SIGHT

DONDIS, DONIS A. *A Primer of Visual Literacy.* Cambridge, Mass.: MIT Press, 1973.

ZETTL, HERBERT. *Sight—Sound—Motion.* Belmont, Calif.: Wadsworth, 1973.

PART FIVE

PRESENTING YOURSELF ON TELEVISION

KEY: 0 = Item does not apply
       1 = Extremely well done
       2 = Fairly well done
       3 = Moderately well done
       4 = Poorly done; needs improvement

CHAPTER 10. Visual Presentation

A. Understood the elements of sight (in general)	0	1	2	3	4
1. Understood color	0	1	2	3	4
2. Understood line	0	1	2	3	4
3. Understood motion	0	1	2	3	4
B. Visual effectiveness (in general)	0	1	2	3	4
1. Use of posture	0	1	2	3	4
2. Use of movement	0	1	2	3	4
3. Use of facial expressions	0	1	2	3	4
4. Use of eye contact	0	1	2	3	4
a. Use of memory aids	0	1	2	3	4
i. Use of notes	0	1	2	3	4
ii. Use of TelePrompTer	0	1	2	3	4

CHAPTER 11. Sound Presentation

A. Use of the elements of sound (in general)	0	1	2	3	4
1. Use of volume	0	1	2	3	4
2. Use of articulation	0	1	2	3	4
3. Use of rate	0	1	2	3	4
4. Use of pitch	0	1	2	3	4
B. Use of microphones (in general)	0	1	2	3	4
1. Use of correct sounds	0	1	2	3	4
2. Use of authentic test	0	1	2	3	4
3. Use of distracting noises	0	1	2	3	4
4. Correct distance from microphones	0	1	2	3	4
C. Controlling nervousness (in general)	0	1	2	3	4
1. Before the production	0	1	2	3	4
2. During the production	0	1	2	3	4
3. After the production	0	1	2	3	4
D. Improving television delivery	0	1	2	3	4
1. Practiced	0	1	2	3	4
2. Reviewed	0	1	2	3	4
3. Sought advice	0	1	2	3	4
4. Located and developed models	0	1	2	3	4
5. Experimented	0	1	2	3	4

PART
SIX

TELEVISION
INTERVIEWS

*To listen closely and reply well is the highest perfection
we are able to attain in the art of conversation.*

La Rochefoucauld

Thus far we have focused on those principles of television communication that fit a variety of situations and programs. We now shift to a specific form—in fact, one of the most commonly experienced forms—of television: the interview.

In Chapter 12 we discuss how to prepare for being interviewed on television. In our own experience and in watching other people, we have observed that lack of preparation is generally devastating to the presentation. We hope Chapter 12 will help you avoid this kind of embarrassment.

In Chapter 13 we talk about actually being interviewed. We have found interaction, questions, and control to be three central elements of television interviews. In this chapter we offer guidelines for dealing with these three elements.

PART
SIX

12. PREPARING FOR THE TELEVISION INTERVIEW

We have experienced some rough moments in television interviews (the time our guest hardly talked to us once the program started), and have watched other people barely make it through an interview. In most instances, the problem could be traced to a lack of preparation. While much of what we have to say about interview preparation applies to both the interviewer and the interviewee, our focus is on the interviewee, the person being interviewed.

We begin by identifying three common types of interviews: press, hosted, and mediated, then go on to discuss five common characteristics of interviews: purpose, organization, interaction, questioning, and control. We conclude this chapter by offering some advice that should make your preparation more productive.

TYPES OF TELEVISION INTERVIEWS

Everyone, at one time or another, will probably participate in an employment, evaluation, counseling, complaint, or other form of interview. While we might soon see the day when television is used for all types of interviews, the three principal types of television interviews you are most likely to be a part of now are press, hosted, and mediated.

Press Interview

Perhaps the most prevalent form of interview on television, the press interview involves one or more members of a television news department asking you questions. The interview can focus on a specific topic (on Monday the government accused your company of dumping waste materials in the bay) or it can be on a general theme (you have just been appointed to the school board and the press wants to know your philosophy). In either case, the interview might be brief or extended, hostile or friendly, in the studio or on location.

Press interviews can be tough, particularly when the element of surprise is brought into play. Several years ago one of the authors was involved in a fairly heated political issue. Suddenly, while up to his neck in cement, building a rock wall in his front yard, he was surrounded by a field reporter and numerous technicians carrying television equipment. What was worse, the reporter had a strong position on the issue and was armed with a series of closed-ended and leading questions (these kinds of questions will be discussed in the next chapter). The lack of opportunity to prepare made that particular press interview incredibly difficult.

Hosted Interview (Talk Shows)

The Johnny Carson, Merv Griffin, Phil Donahue, and Dick Cavett shows are but a few of the interview programs broadcast on commercial, educational, cable, and closed-circuit television. You may have engineered your appearance on a hosted interview, unlike many press interviews, or you may have been asked to appear.

Generally taking place in a studio, a hosted interview is often longer than a press interview. Not only are more questions asked, but you can plan on taking more time to answer them. A hosted interview is less likely to be hostile compared to a press interview. A press interview can catch you by surprise; a hosted interview generally gives you plenty of time to prepare.

Mediated Interview

In mediated interviews the people involved are not in the same place— they each talk to a camera and see the other in a monitor. Ted Koppel's

Figure 12.1 A hosted interview.
The host (on the left) checks his notes while the guest responds to a question. The director most likely has chosen the view from Camera 2 to allow the host "privacy" for his preparations. Photography by Scott Highton. Courtesy of Over Easy/KQED.

Nightline is an example of the mediated interview. And we've all seen this form of interview in network news, when the anchor person talks to a reporter on location. Such interviews are becoming increasingly common.

Teleconferencing is yet another type of mediated interview. The interviewee and the interviewer are in two different studios and can "broadcast" questions and answers to each other. By means of these conferences, personnel directors in New York can interview job applicants in Detroit or San Diego. A medical expert can be in a studio in Denver and be asked questions by patients or doctors who are in studios and medical facilities throughout the United States and the world.

In some ways it is easier to do a press or hosted interview than a mediated interview. Speaking directly to a camera is difficult and takes practice.

CHARACTERISTICS OF TELEVISION INTERVIEWS

All interviews, regardless of the specific type or format, share a set of characteristics that differentiate them from other forms of communication. Understanding these characteristics, and how they influence the communication process, might well be the first step you should take in preparing for television interviews.

Purpose

People often assume that because the interview is set up like a casual conversation ("just two people sitting around talking"), it is random and aimless. This assumption is not true. When you're being interviewed on television, the reporter, talk-show host, or personnel director has a specific goal in mind. It isn't by chance that you're on camera. Someone believed that you had something to say and created a situation in which you could say it. Knowing the reason you're on television will help you prepare and participate more effectively.

Organization

While good interviewers give the illusion of being spontaneous, they actually know well in advance what questions they're going to ask. They usually even know the sequence of the questions. The next time you watch *The Tonight Show* or *Meet the Press,* notice how the interviewers refer to notes on their desks. These notes help them conduct the interview in an organized fashion while also allowing them a degree of flexibility.

The Exchange of Interactive Messages

The interviewer and the interviewee are engaged in a shared communication event. Both have responsibilities. They take turns speaking and listening; they are independent and respond directly to each other in light of what is transpiring. This simultaneous involvement, on both a verbal and nonverbal level, means that neither party can remain silent or anonymous. When someone asks you, "What does your company plan to do now that it has been charged with sexual discrimination?" you are part of a message exchange that can't be avoided. You must listen and speak. We will talk about both of these activities in greater length in the next chapter.

Questions

From your own experiences it should be obvious that the question supplies that power that keeps the interview moving. Regardless of the goal or setting, the interviewer asks questions that must be answered. This, of course, is very different from most of our daily face-to-face experiences where we can ask as well as answer questions. While there are occasions when the interviewee might ask a question (asking clarification to a question, and so on), it is the interviewer who sets the tone by the questions he or she selects.

Control

In most television productions, a script is written, a director gives orders, and everyone knows his or her part. In interviews, there is often a clash of wills. The questioner may have one goal, while the person answering may have a different goal. In the final analysis, it is the interviewer who generally controls the interview. But in the next chapter we will talk about ways that you, as the interviewee, can exercise some control as well.

THE SYSTEMATIC APPROACH

The television interview, like all appearances on television, actually begins long before the cameras roll. While you can never anticipate everything that will happen during the interview, you can, by thorough preparation, have a general idea of the questions and issues you will face. Talk-show hosts and newspersons do their homework—so must you. Admittedly, the level of preparation depends on the situation. Having a microphone thrust in front of you as you leave a polling booth is not the same as preparing to defend your company's policy to a group of stockholders who are going to quiz you via a closed-circuit system.

We recommend a systematic approach in preparing for television interviews, involving the following six steps:

1. Learn all you can about the interview.

2. Know what you want to say (your main purpose).

3. Prepare some possible responses.

4. Know your rights and exercise them.

5. Practice.

6. Prepare physically and mentally.

Learn All You Can

This simple-sounding bit of advice actually involves a great many chores. It is based on the assumption that you should not go to the interview expecting to play a passive role. Rather, you should anticipate an exchange of ideas, and many of the ideas should be yours.

The answers to the following questions should give you some insight into what the interview will be like and how you should behave.

1. *What is the purpose of the interview?* Why the program is being broadcast affects nearly every phase of the interview. It tells you first and foremost why *you* are there. Are you appearing to entertain, inform, persuade, or all three? You need to know this if you hope to be able to exercise some control over the flow of the interview.

2. *What type of interview will it be?* Knowing the specific format gives you an idea of what questions you might be asked, how long you will have to answer them, and how many other people will be with you.

3. *Why have I been selected to appear on this interview show?* There is a reason the producer, news director, or talk-show host asked for you. And that reason, be it your position, expertise, or personality, will influence the type of questions you will be asked, and, of course, the answers you give.

4. *Who will be conducting the interview?* Is the questioner a popular member of the community or a newscaster with a reputation for treating interviewees in a hostile manner? Knowing the communication style of the person asking the questions will help you determine what you can expect once the camera is turned on. Try to see the interviewer in action *before* the program. You might even talk to people who have been questioned by him or her. If possible, try to find out what the interviewer knows about you and your subject. Is the interviewer the expert or are you?

5. *What is the technical and physical setting of the interview?* Will the program be taped or live? In the studio or on location? Will there be chairs, desks, or couches? Will I be alone or sharing the set with other people? What sort of makeup and wardrobe demands will be placed on me?

6. *How long will the interview be?* Think for a moment about the type and amount of preparation you would need for a three-minute interview versus a one-hour appearance on a talk show. The depth of your research is bound to be influenced by this question.

7. *Who will the audience be?* The answer to this question, as much as any other, has a ripple effect that is felt in a number of areas. In choosing everything from vocabulary to visual aids, the audience must be taken into account. A small, specialized cable audience is not the same as the homogeneous population that watches network news. Knowing the differences among audiences must be part of your preparation.

Know What You Want To Say

This piece of advice might seem contradictory, since interviewing is spontaneous and the questions asked can be off the cuff. But having a clear sense of your main purpose before the interview begins can help you immeasurably.

In a typical interview, the respondent talks approximately 70 percent of the time. In this time you should try to get your key points across. That means you must identify your purpose during the preparation process. If you don't, you're apt to ramble, get frustrated, and even make a fool of yourself.

Jack Hilton and Mary Knoblauch, experienced television personalities, underscore the importance of deciding your purpose—and then accomplishing it—in their book *On Television*. After discussing one of his appearances on television, Hilton wrote, "I went away [from that experience] with one lesson firmly learned, and being interviewed on television has never bothered me since that day. The lesson is: Know what you want to say, and use whatever questions you are asked to say it."[1]

Prepare Some Responses

We now move from simply identifying your purpose to deciding on some practical ways to see that it is achieved: becoming knowledgeable on the topic, gathering concrete evidence, and selecting examples, stories, and anecdotes. Preparing your response also means thinking about some problems you might face and developing contingency plans.

When preparing some possible responses, remember that you may not be given as much time as you would like to make your case, so practice explaining what you want to say in as few words as possible. You can develop this technique by saying to yourself before the interview, "If I can get only one thing across, what should it be?" Once that question has been answered, you can begin to think about how you can articulate that point clearly and concisely as soon as the opportunity presents itself.

Suggest Your Introduction

In most instances, before the taping begins, the producer or interviewer will ask you how you would like to be introduced. We urge you to take advantage of this request. You might even volunteer some input about your introduction if the production staff fails to contact you before airtime.

The introduction has two main purposes: to acquaint the audience with you and to arouse interest in what you will be talking about. To see that you and your message receive a favorable reception, you and the person introducing you should follow a few simple guidelines.

1. Ask him or her to be brief. In a good-natured way you can let the introducer know that you don't want a ten-minute speech before you get a chance to talk. Such wordy introductions are boring and often embarrassing.

2. Give the introducer some information that can establish your credibility on the topic, such as your titles, honors, positions, background on the topic, and the reason you are on television.

3. Make sure that the information you give the introducer is accurate. This advice applies not only to your personal data, but also to the correct pronunciation of your name. We have seen interviews start off poorly because the person being interviewed had to correct the host before answering the first question.

Be Assertive

As we have said, too many novice performers let the experience of being on television intimidate them. Not only are they overwhelmed by the mere idea of performing, but they behave as if someone very powerful were doing them a great favor by allowing them to appear in front of a camera. Both of these notions should be rejected. Don't be intimidated; don't be servile. Assert yourself when necessary, politely yet firmly.

This assertiveness should be reflected in your willingness to ask some questions of the producer, production staff, and interviewer. Here is a brief list of some of the questions you might ask:

1. Can you meet with the interviewer before airtime?

2. Can you have an idea of the type of questions that will be asked?

3. In an employment interview, can you be assured that the questions will not be illegal and/or an invasion of your privacy? (Questions that discriminate on the basis of race, sex, religion, or national origin fall into this category.)

4. Will you be able to use notes? If not, why?

5. Will you be able to use visual aids? If not, why?

6. Will you be furnished with a written or video transcript of the interview?

7. Can you be informed of the basic ground rules—time, location, personnel, equipment, right of veto, right to edit, and so on?

Practice, Practice, Practice

It has been said that success is nine-tenths practice; we would agree. Preparing for the television interview must, whenever possible, include some practice sessions. Granted, it is hard to practice for an interview if a news crew walks into your office unannounced and starts firing questions at you. But in most cases you will have some advance notice and can use this time to work on the following points.

Rehearse some possible questions and answers. You might ask a colleague to serve as the interviewer and help you construct a mock program. By drafting questions and working on suitable replies, you can talk through the major issues before airtime. When preparing for political interviews, most candidates will spend an entire day cloistered with their staff, fielding potential questions as if they were actually on television. Even the president of the United States spends hours having his aides ask him questions before he meets with the press.

Make your practice session as realistic as possible. If you plan to use notecards or a clipboard during your actual performance, use them when you practice. If possible, use the same type of equipment that you will face in the studio. Videotaping the practice session and viewing it later is particularly helpful.

In Chapter 10 we stressed the importance of your physical appearance before the camera. A quick review of that chapter could help you prepare for a television interview. As with most aspects of television, your clothing, jewelry, makeup, and the like can be decided on well in advance of the actual presentation.

Although we mention it last, preparing mentally is the most crucial phase of preparing for a television interview: Develop a positive attitude about yourself and your subject, and then clear your mind of all matters other than the interview. These two points are not as easy as they sound. The key to both, we believe, is looking forward to the television experience with enthusiasm, not fear.

13. BEING INTERVIEWED ON TELEVISION

Having emphasized the importance of preparing for television interviews, we now discuss three principles you should understand while doing a television interview: interaction, questioning and control.

INTERACTION

In Chapter 2 we talked about intrapersonal, interpersonal, group, public, and mass forms of communication. An interview is interpersonal, a form of communication involving very few people and some sense of interaction.

In an interview, interaction is of the essence. Interaction involves two primary activities, listening and speaking. What we offer here are fifteen suggestions, based on common sense and good manners, for productive listening and speaking in a television interview.

Listening

We begin not, as you might expect, with some advice on talking, but on listening. If you don't hear the question, you can't supply the answer.

We've seen countless examples of people who did poorly in press conferences and on talk shows simply because they didn't listen. While listening is too complex to be adequately treated in a few pages, we can suggest a number of do's and don'ts that will improve the way you hear and
subsequently respond to the questions you're asked.

1. *Start listening from the outset.* One of the most common errors
   made in listening is not being prepared to listen. You may be
   thinking about how you look, how you sound, or who's watching, just as the interviewer begins to ask the question. It's crucial that you clear your mind and, if possible, your environment
   from all distraction before the first question is asked. If you're
   adjusting your microphone or worrying about whether you have
   enough makeup on, you may not hear all of the nuances of the
   question. Remember, just a couple of words can alter the entire
   idea behind the question. Being asked about a specific 1982
   court ruling on capital punishment is not the same as being
   asked to comment on capital punishment in general. Not paying
   attention to this type of difference can cause you serious embarrassment.

2. *Don't fake attention.* Our culture puts a premium on being polite, and part of being polite is looking attentive. However, appearing to listen is not the same as truly listening. Many listeners are so busy exhibiting the outward signs of listening
   (smiling, nodding) that they forget to concentrate on the content
   of the question. This is especially true in television. While we
   wouldn't disparage the importance of appearance on television,
   we would nevertheless urge you not to let faking attention get
   in the way of sincere and conscientious listening.

3. *Be aware that you can think faster than the interviewer can
   talk.* We speak at an average rate of 125 to 150 words per
   minute. Yet it's estimated that the brain can process approximately 400 words per minute. What we do with this spare time
   is bound to vary from person to person. We've found, though,
   that when we asked people what they're doing instead of listening, their responses fell into two categories.
      One group, instead of listening to the entire question, be-
   gins to work on their answer. This is a big mistake, for while
   you're constructing a clever retort or rebuttal, the interviewer
   is likely to add some essential information that you'll miss.
   Learn to suspend working on your answer until you've heard
   the entire question.

The other group focuses on the interviewer's delivery—*how* the question is asked, instead of *what* is being asked. This is an easy trap to fall into. Because you're nervous, you're apt to be easily mesmerized by the interviewer's voice. But when the talking stops, you'll realize with some consternation that you have no idea what was said. Try to stay alert.

4. *Whenever necessary, take notes.* If the format allows for it, you should be prepared to take notes as the interviewer asks the question. This means having paper and pencil ready *before* you start listening. Next time you see William F. Buckley being interviewed, notice that he takes notes as he listens.

   One brief word of caution: Note-taking is no simple matter. Not only is it difficult to do, but you run the risk of having some of your viewers perceive it as rude. With practice, and with short questions and responses, you may eventually reach a point where you don't need notes. However, if you need to take notes, there are three things to keep in mind.

   First, don't stop listening just because you're writing. Remember, the brain can handle writing and listening at the same time. Second, make sure your notes can be used once you need them. Being lackadaisical in your note-taking can render your notes useless as you move from the role of listener to speaker. Third, keep your notes brief. Long, involved notes will be hard to use. List a few key words that will act as triggers for your memory.

5. *Try to identify the main point of the question.* A question usually has a specific purpose. While each word is important, it is this central idea that must be identified. If an interviewer traces the history of your company's stance on air pollution, and then finishes with a question about what's going on now, you should, unless some false facts were presented, talk about the present situation—that is the main point of the question.

6. *Be motivated to listen.* We've saved our most important suggestion for last. For if you can be motivated to listen you will be able to overcome many of the problems of listening we alluded to in the last few pages. If you can find a reason to pay attention you will be more alert to what is being discussed; you will also be less prone to yield to distractions.

   We should add that telling you to be motivated as a listener is a much simpler task than telling you *how* to be motivated. Because motivation is highly subjective and situational, one particular recommendation does not apply to all people or all situations. *You* must decide on a reason to pay attention. These reasons can range from the practical ("If I listen, I'll be able to hire the right person for our company."), to the philosophical ("I owe it to the other person to listen—I'd like her to listen to me."). Regardless of the reason, being motivated will improve your communication behavior.

Speaking

You will see from our discussion of the following suggestions that, as with listening, speaking in a television interview is largely a matter of common sense. But, as Emerson observed, "Common sense is often as rare as genius."

1. *State your main point first.* By getting your thesis on the floor early, it'll be there even if you're interrupted or cut off. Unlike newspaper interviews, which are much longer, the television interview can be terminated quickly if the interviewer thinks you're uninteresting or taking too long to answer the question. The interviewer can even ask you another question while you're in the middle of your first response. So get to your main point as soon as possible.

   If asked what the school board planned to do about the new court ruling on busing, you can't take time to say, "I have ten points to cover as I try to answer your question. First, ..." Your response has to be pointed: "We have bought fourteen new buses, hired drivers, and we will start carrying out the new busing program this Monday."

2. *Be brief.* In Ecclesiasticus, the following advice was given: "Let thy speech be short, comprehending much in few words." This wisdom applies today. Brevity is crucial in television presentations. Television is ruled by the clock and it thrives on speed. This combination discourages long-winded responses.

   This idea was made clear in a recent article in *Time* magazine, which noted that television's formula for news interviews these days is perhaps 100 words from the reporter, and a "sound bite" of 15–20 words from the interviewee. "In these days of short attention spans and mandatory commercial breaks, . . . those with little to say come through better, . . . and those with a lot to say have a hard time."[2]

   Some of your interviews might be only forty seconds long, while others could last an hour or more. Yet in all instances you should make your answers brief. Following this simple rule will not only help you get your main point across, but will also keep you from wasting time with needless pauses and digressions. Trying to fill time often leads to fillers such as "well . . . ," "um . . . ," and "er . . . ." It can also lead to what is often called "foot-in-mouth disease." Notice as you watch press conferences how many journalists will seize on an idea that was just tossed out by mistake. Therefore, say what you want to say, and then be still.

3. *Relate to your audience.* A major difference between print and television interviews serves as the rationale for this suggestion. Newspaper reporters interpret, synthesize, condense, and even illuminate your comments. They mediate between you and your receivers. This is not the case with television interviews. When you appear on television, there's no go-between. Your message and image are being perceived directly by the person watching the set.

Because of this immediacy, we suggest that you adapt your delivery in two ways. First, strive for an air of informality. Remember, in most instances you are going into someone's home or office. Use a conversational tone. Too many novices are artificial and try to model themselves after someone they've seen on television; you are not Barbara Walters or Phil Donahue. Work on conveying some simple human traits such as courtesy, conviction, tact, and sincerity.

Second, your relationship to the audience should even be reflected in your physical presentation. Try to appear alert, interested, and enthusiastic, by varying your rate, volume, and pitch; maintaining a comfortable and natural posture; smiling when appropriate; and looking at the interviewer. Remember that eye contact is important. You will look foolish and uninterested if you search for the tally light and can't find it. To avoid getting caught looking at the wrong camera, think of the person asking the questions as both the camera and the viewer watching you at home. In this way you can avoid being embarrassed and maintain your relationship with the audience.

4. *Be accurate.* While this advice would seem to go without saying, we would be remiss if we didn't remind you of your obligation to be accurate and truthful when you state your facts and figures. All of your preparation and good intentions are fruitless if you distort your information. Not only is it unethical, but such statements will harm you and your cause. The trained interviewer will ferret out an error in your presentation

and quickly exploit your blunder. This blunder, regardless of
how innocent or unintentional, can even be the stimulus for a
libel suit. That is to say, should you offer false information or
simply not be accurate, you might find yourself moving from
the television studio to the courtroom. Check your facts, keep
them at your fingertips, and use them accurately when they
apply.

5. *Don't flaunt your expertise.* If you have done a great deal of research, and know your subject thoroughly, you may find it hard
   to repress an air of smugness. But seeming self-satisfied can
   only hurt you. Being smug in your facial expressions, tone of
   voice, or use of examples could easily turn the interviewer and
   the audience against you.
       We should add that there are two reasons that it's easy to
   slip into an attitude that communicates vanity. First, when you
   have spent weeks or months gathering your data and practicing
   its delivery, wanting to dazzle the interviewer is quite under-
   standable. You have worked hard and in one way or another everyone is going to know it. Try not to give in to this tendency.
   Be frustrated, but don't parade your knowledge if it is only for
   your ego.
       Second, it's tempting to flaunt your expertise when you're
   being interviewed by someone who isn't well informed—and this
   is not uncommon. Being a talk-show host, personnel director, or
   reporter doesn't mean that a person is knowledgeable in all
   areas. Many first-time interviewees overreact when they discover that they know more than the person asking the questions, and display, in obvious ways, just how much they know.
   We urge you not to give in to this tendency. The viewers may
   find you obnoxious. When you feel yourself yielding to the urge
   to show off, remember the words of Sir Walter Scott: "Education
   is like a fine watch. It should be taken out only at those moments when there is a need for it."

6. *Don't be evasive.* Much of what you see on network television
   could lead you to believe that television viewers are not very intelligent. However, this is not true. Not everyone sits around
   and watches situation comedies all day and night. Most viewers
   are perceptive enough to know if your answer to a question is
   evasive. Evasiveness, shown by words or actions, is often taken
   as a form of deception—and you know how much people dislike
   being duped. Don't be afraid to ask for more information or to
   say, "Sorry, but I don't know the answer to that question." There
   are a variety of ways to say "I don't know." You can try "I don't

have that information now but I'll try to get it." Or "I'm sorry, but I can't answer that question right now. I simply don't have the answer." In both of these instances you are not being evasive. You are also avoiding the rather dramatic and overused "No comment!", which sounds brusque and insincere.

7. *Stay calm—even during difficult times.* Even when watching the news, people want to be entertained. Many television interviewers, be they reporters or talk-show hosts, are aware of this fact and enjoy nothing more than goading you with loaded questions into losing your temper and saying the wrong thing. They believe that anger and faux pas have entertainment value. They may be right, but there is no reason that you should be the one to prove it. Stay calm.

Many beginning interviewees get nervous during lulls in the conversation and show signs of strain. The interviewer is asking the questions; if there is intense silence, let him or her worry about it. Don't react to the silence by reiterating your previous comments, muttering, or fidgeting. The silence may well be a ploy to make you feel uncomfortable.

Finally, staying calm also means not acting defensive when you're provoked. Keep your temper, remain civil, and the audience will side with you. In fact, a good technique is to soften your answers as the questions become more aggressive. This gives the impression of being poised and relaxed, in contrast with the hard, abrasive interviewer. Remember, television thrives on controversy. Many of the interviewers you'll meet will try to create controversy at your expense. Be careful!

8. *Make effective use of language.* In Chapter 7 we noted that every profession has its own specialized language, a code known to its members but often confusing to outsiders. To some extent, everyone may speak a jargon that is unfamiliar to the viewer. *Interface, encoding and decoding, feedback,* and *cognitive dissonance–consonance* may have meaning to the communications professor, but not to most other people. We aren't suggesting that you talk down to your viewers, but that you learn to modify your language just enough so that they'll understand it. It is even a good technique to use the device of paraphrasing as a means of making sure the interviewer doesn't overuse jargon. If he isn't clear, you can help your viewers by tactfully saying to him, "Let me reword your question to see if I understand it."

Effective language is also characterized by accuracy. Select your words with care. Say exactly what you mean, in words that are specific and concrete. Use names, dates, facts, and other details to make your ideas specific. Notice how accurate words could improve the following two sentences: "*Lots* of people are on welfare." "*This thing* happens all the time." Such careless use of language does not contribute to clear communication.

When answering questions, try to use language that is vivid. Vividness serves a variety of purposes. It can help capture attention, maintain interest, and contribute to your credibility.

Making your answers more vivid often is as simple as learning how to use descriptive adjectives and adverbs. Phrases such as "a chilling adventure," "a contemplative and thoughtful professor," "a sarcastic response" offer the listener a more complete image of what is being talked about.

Using language well also means avoiding unnecessary verbal distractions. Too often, because of laziness or a lack of training, people will express themselves in ways that call attention to their sloppy language. Let's look at a few types of words and phrases that can detract from your purpose.

Slang might be appropriate when talking with friends, but it can only hurt your cause when you use it on television. What would be your impression of a speaker who used expressions such as *freaked out; busted; bombed; bummer; bad vibes; super; into; for sure*?

Closely related to slang are clichés. A **cliché** is a phrase that is lacking in imagination, creativity, and even clarity. We again ask you to speculate on the image you would form of a speaker whose style was characterized by some of the following: *sharp as a tack; dead as a doornail; cool as a cucumber; hit the nail on the head; better late than never; behind the eight ball; as American as apple pie; talk is cheap.*

9. *Try to establish and maintain your personal credibility.* The studio, through its equipment and personnel, may affect the credibility of the program and even what the viewers think of you. But what can you yourself do to enhance your image?

   a. If you're **experienced** in a subject, and that's why you're being interviewed, that experience gives you credibility with your audience. You don't need to brag about it, but you would be remiss not to give your interviewer a thorough accounting of your experience. This accounting might take place during the rehearsal period *before* the program begins so that the interviewer can ask you specific questions that will demonstrate your expertise. This is to say, if you have traveled to China, and the topic under discussion is Oriental art, the host should ask you some questions about your trip. If he or she fails to do so, you should try to work the point gracefully into the conversation.

b. Your **use of information** is another way of demonstrating your credibility. Showing you know the facts will give your television presentation authority. Having the facts is a matter of knowing what someone in your position should know, and perhaps a bit more. Think about how credible you would appear if, speaking on the subject of prayers in school, you verbally traced all the major court decisions concerning this topic.

c. You can establish credibility by **being reasonable.** As we noted in Chapter 4, reason is as essential to television as it is to everyday conversation. We trust people who are logical and appear to have given some thought to their presentation.

   Organization, as we point out in Part Three, is important in television communication. If you're being interviewed and can't find your notes, you look scatterbrained. If you're hosting an interview and get cut off because a commercial caught you unawares, you lose a bit of credibility in the eyes of an experienced television audience (and most television audiences are very experienced in watching television).

d. **Integrity** is another element of credibility. Though we may not have liked the news Walter Cronkite brought us, there was an integrity to his news reports. *Trustworthiness, integrity, ethics, honesty,* and *fairness* all cluster around the notion of credibility.

e. Being **empathetic** with and relating to your audience can help your credibility. The more you can associate yourself with the general human condition, the better able you should be to exhibit your good will toward your audience. All of us have respect for the person who seems to be interested in the well-being of others.

f. Similarly, credibility can be manifested through **identification.** If you can make the audience see that you are like them, you add to your credibility. Johnny Carson's stories of his childhood, for example, allow the audience to identify with his roots and his background.

Credibility is essential to communication. Chrysler could try to sell cars by showing the product and reiterating specifications. But Lee Iacocca lends the Chrysler pitch a personal touch. He brings experience, organization, and other forms of good sense to his presentation of the Chrysler product. He vouches for the product and lends it his stamp of integrity. He conveys good will by personally relating to the audience, showing concern for their happiness with the Chrysler product. Lee Iacocca lends good sense, moral character, and good will to a mass of mechanical and electronic components. As the source of a television message, you do no less; you bring character to what otherwise might be a cold and dull message.

TYPES OF QUESTIONS

If you watch television interviews and listen to the questions, you know that they take a number of different forms. Open-ended, closed-ended, hypothetical, probing, and silent questions are the ones most often used in television interviews. Knowing these types of questions can help you plan your strategy and also word your answers. Let's look at these types of questions so that you will recognize them when they are asked.

Open-Ended Questions

These are very popular in television interviews. Their widespread use stems from the fact that they are general, broad, unstructured, and allow for some latitude in the answers they are soliciting. Notice the freedom the interviewee is given with the following open-ended questions: "Tell me about yourself." "What things did you like about China?" "What steps would you take to solve this current problem?" "How did you happen to come up with this idea?"

Some news interviewers stay away from the open question, because they believe that it takes more time to answer. They're also leery of the ease with which the untrained respondent can begin to ramble when asked an open question. As an interviewee, your eyes should light up when the interviewer decides to overlook these two reservations and asks you an open-ended question. Being able to choose what you want to say should help you get your point across.

Closed-Ended Questions

The answer you are allowed to offer to the closed question is limited. How much elaboration can you offer if someone asks you, "What was your major in college?" "How many times have you appeared on television?" Some closed questions, used mainly by journalists, are answered with a simple yes or no. Here are some examples: "Did you come here directly from the hospital?" "Did you have a role in deciding on this current plan?" Experienced performers know they are not on trial; they often give other responses to closed questions: "The issue is much too complex for me to give you a yes-or-no answer. Let me offer you an explanation of what really happened."

Many talk-show hosts avoid closed-ended questions because they lead to dull conversation. However, you're likely to find them used by television news people, potential employers, and people who are asking you questions via an interactive talk-back system.

Hypothetical Questions

Hypothetical questions are those that are based on imaginary situations; hence they call for imaginary answers. At a news conference a reporter might ask, "What would you do if the blacks in your factory started to picket because of on-the-job discrimination?" As you can see, this example asks for a hypothetical response. Yet your response might be "Our company doesn't engage in any form of discrimination, so your question doesn't apply to us."

In less formal situations, where entertainment is as much the goal as information, the hypothetical question can be fun. You can use humor and lively examples when the host asks you "What would you do if you had my job?"

Leading Questions

Be careful of questions phrased so that, implicitly or explicitly, you have to answer a certain way. (Our hypothetical example about racial discrimination could be considered a leading question.) Notice the potential trap in the following questions: "When was the last time you missed one of these important meetings?" "You would vote for capital punishment, wouldn't you?" "Most of the people who have researched this issue believe that Mr. Jones was wrong. Don't you?" "You don't steal anymore, do you?"

These types of questions, like closed questions, are of limited value in most interviews, so you are likely to face them in only a few isolated situations. However, when you do detect a leading question, don't be tricked into answering it. It's often a good technique to tell the interviewer, in a calm voice, that you would like to offer your own views on the topic and not use hers. Remember, there aren't any embarrassing questions—just embarrassing answers. So don't give one.

Probes

The probe comes into play when the interviewer is not satisfied with your answer and wants more depth, more evidence, or clarification of a point. Sometimes, of course, the probe is used to stir up controversy.

The **elaboration** or clarification probe asks you to explain some or part of your answer to a question in more detail.

> Question: *Why did you decide to vote against the new park on the east side of town?*
> Answer: *Lots of reasons.*
> Probe: *Can you give us a few of these?*

The interviewer might directly **restate** your response; this is also a probe to get you to say more on the topic.

> Question: *What do you like best about your company's current position on this issue?*
> Answer: *The lack of corporate trivia.*
> Probe: *You like the lack of corporate trivia?*

In the **paraphrase** probe, the interviewer repeats the original question in slightly different words to get you to respond.

> Question: *What do you think we should do about the new high-speed bullet train being proposed for our area?*
> Answer: *This is a very complex issue. One must think of the environmental impact, the financial ramifications, and whether there is a need for such a project.*
> Probe: *Knowing that there are lots of problems, what do you suggest?*

Silence is also used as a form of questioning. Novice interviewees usually have a low tolerance for dead air, and will add to their answer if the interviewer doesn't immediately respond.

> Question: *Why did you decide to run for the school board?*
> Answer: *I saw a great many problems facing our district.*
> Probe: *(Silence)*

The silent treatment can involve a number of paraverbal fillers. "Hmmm," "Oh yes," "Okay," "I see," and "Uh-huh" are all intended to tell you to go on with what you're talking about. Even smiling and nodding encourages further conversation.

The Sequence of Questions

Very few interviewers will ask their questions at random. Usually they'll have an overall organizational scheme for the entire interview and also have a plan for each series of questions. The narrower sequences can be classified as the funnel and inverted funnel techniques.

The **funnel** sequence begins with general or broad questions and then moves the focus to more specific issues. It is often a movement from open to closed questions. For example: "Why do you think your school district let this happen? How many people were involved in this decision? Were the administrators acting on their own? Did they consult with the teachers?"

In the **inverted funnel** sequence, the questions start specific, then become more general as the interview progresses. For example: "Did you vote against the new park? Had you voted against any other recreational projects in the last year? Which ones? Why? What is your feeling about the government supplying recreation facilities for its citizens? Can you give us your personal philosophy regarding the role of government in offering people a 'better life'?"

In either case, recognizing the sequence is to your advantage. It helps you plan your strategy.

CONTROL IN TELEVISION INTERVIEWS

Control is difficult to establish in a television interview because there are at least two people involved, each capable of speaking and listening, each susceptible to questioning and answering. You may not have control over the person interviewing you, or over the way the program is produced and edited, but you can control yourself, your message, and how interesting you are.

Controlling Yourself

In Chapter 11 we talked about the physiological manifestations of anxiety; we also suggested ways to alleviate anxiety. As we noted, it takes self-control to deal with such problems. In discussing the interactive nature of television interviews, we mentioned a number of general rules for speaking and listening; it takes self-control to observe and follow those rules. From the moment you accept an interview to the moment the interview is over, your principal task is self-control.

Your responsibility for control may also include the equipment, the person interviewing you, and even your audience. Your primary responsibilities beyond yourself, however, involve your message and your interest level.

Controlling the Message

Because the interviewer asks most of the questions, it might be difficult, at times, to adhere to the advice we're offering here. Yet it's crucial for you *not* to let the interviewer put words in your mouth, cut you off while talking, ask too many leading questions, and otherwise dominate the flow of the interview. Remember, the interviewer wants to be perceived as stimulating and intelligent, and may try to accomplish this goal by controlling every aspect of the interaction. There are, however, a number of things you can do to see to it that you have some influence over what happens.

1. Make sure you come to the interview well informed. If you're firmly grounded in the facts, you'll be able to identify which questions are being asked to bait you and which are legitimate.

2. You can influence the flow of the interview by asking questions of the interviewer. Nowhere is it chiseled in stone that only interviewers ask questions. You might ask for more details and/or clarification ("Can you please be more specific as to the year you're talking about?") Some experienced television performers can even follow up one question with yet another: "Are you sure you have the date right?"

3. While you might be the "guest," you can still be assertive about not allowing the interviewer to interrupt you. Try not to become too abrasive as you respond to interruptions; comments such as "Could I please finish my answer?" often have an effect opposite what is intended.

    You can preclude interruption by raising your voice. Often just the slightest increase in volume can tell the interviewer you want to finish. The degree of tact you employ is obviously related to the spirit of the interruption and your relationship with the interviewer. But regardless of the circumstances, keep control of the interview by not allowing the interviewer's interruptions to go unchecked.

4. Steering the course of the interview also involves refuting incorrect statements and not letting yourself be misinterpreted. Refutation should be immediate; if incorrect statements are al-

lowed to stand, they will be taken as fact. Let's say your
company fired two union organizers last year, and the interviewer says to you, "Last year your company fired six people because they tried to start a labor union. How will you approach
the NLRB hearings?" Before you respond to the question, you
need to correct the facts.

5. Learning how to use transitions will greatly aid you in your efforts to control the interview. Let's look at a few transitional devices that work well in television interviews.

   a. **Bridging,** perhaps one of the most popular transitions used
      in interviews, gets you in a sentence or two from what is be-
      ing talked about to where you'd rather be. For example:
      "Why don't we look at the entire picture instead of this small
      portion?" or "There's a little background information that we
      should look at before I can objectively deal with your ques-
      tion."

   b. A **partition,** which previews each point you plan to intro-
      duce, lets you tell the viewer and the interviewer that you
      have a number of things to say. By noting, in advance, that
      you won't be limited to one response, you're controlling the
      interaction. Notice the potential impact of the following par-
      tition: "Let me begin by dividing the question into two parts.
      First allow me a quick response as to how all this trouble
      started, and then I'll turn to my specific solution." A word of
      caution is in order, though. Don't enumerate too many items
      or your audience will lose interest.

   c. **Sign-posting** is the technique of telling your audience what
      your next point will be. For example: "I'll begin answering
      your question by telling you how I feel about this most re-
      cent court ruling." Then as you move to another point: "Now
      let me spend a minute telling you my personal view on this
      issue."

   d. **Paraphrasing** lets you restate the question in a form that
      you find more suited to your purpose. If the interviewer goes
      on at great length about school prayer, and you want to deal
      with only part of the long question, you could say, "If I un-
      derstand your question, you're really asking me what our
      district plans to do about Mr. Jones's having his students
      start their day with the Lord's Prayer."

   e. Finally, transitions can be **nonverbal** as well as verbal.
      Leaning forward, smiling, pausing, moving in one direction

or another all signal that a new point is about to be introduced. And you, not the interviewer, are doing the introducing.

6. Creating a situation that gives you the last word is yet another
way you can control the interview. Interviewers like to wrap
things up neatly before signing off, which is fine—unless you
have something important left to say. Don't get caught with the
tally light blinking off before you've had a chance to make sure
you were understood. In short, don't let the interviewer control
the clock.

Controlling Interest

Some people seem to always be in demand as interviewees. Why? Because they're informed, they speak well, they're honest, and they're *interesting*. Their conversation holds the attention of the viewers—and
this is what interviewers want.

Being interesting is not some magical or innate characteristic; it is
a skill that can be learned. With knowledge and practice, you can
greatly increase your desirability as an interviewee. What are some
things you can do that will make your answers more interesting?

STORIES   The people we like to watch being interviewed on television are
those who know how to tell a good story. They make effective use of illustrations, examples, and anecdotes. Even if your stories and examples
aren't hilarious or profound, they'll hold attention much better than a
simple yes–no answer. Notice how the following illustration in a response
to a question focuses attention while making a point.

Question: *Tell me, Jeff, what got you interested in the pollution
problem now facing Mission Bay?*

Answer: *It's strange how it all started. For years I've had the hobby
of underwater photography. As each year went by, I noticed my pictures were getting darker and darker and I
was seeing fewer fish. At first I thought it was my
equipment and my eyes. But then I started to see more
and more strange objects floating in the water. As I
started to inspect them, I discovered that they were simply pieces of trash that had been dumped in or near the
bay. What was going on was now quite clear. Our lovely
bay was being polluted, and I believe eventually ruined,
by the needless dumping of trash into the water. So I decided to do something about it.*

TIMELINESS   Being interesting also means that you talk about things that are current. People don't want to listen to old news or ideas that they can't relate to. Therefore, you should present up-to-date and pointed information during the interview.

> Question: *How does this issue touch the people in your district?*
> Answer: *Next week the people in our community will be asked to vote on new bonds for a park. If the vote is affirmative, we'll get a playground, new swimming pool, golf course, and several picnic areas. However, should the voters decide on a no vote, we will not only fail to get these things but will have to give back the state's matching funds.*

HUMOR   An old saying has it that "Men will let you fool them if only you will make them laugh." While this might be a slight exaggeration, humor, when tastefully used, can create and maintain interest.

However, humor must be used with great care. Not only does being funny require skill, it also demands a thorough and accurate analysis of the situation and the audience. What one group finds hilarious another might consider offensive. Even sarcasm can hurt your image if it's inappropriate.

Most experts on the subject of humor tell us that amusing examples normally contain one or all of the following ingredients: exaggeration, incongruity, verbal attacks on authority, and self-criticism.

Exaggeration overstates a situation so that it becomes ludicrous. If asked about the size of your company's new in-house television studio, you might respond, "Well, the place is small. In fact, so small that the dog we have to protect it at night has to wag his tail up and down instead of sideways."

Incongruity produces humor because the parts of the situation don't fit together. The unusual, the sudden, the unexpected twist, the inconsistent are all potential sources of humor. Saying that your favorite pastimes are sleeping on a bed of nails, eating raw fish, and appearing on a television talk show could be humorous because of the incongruent sequencing.

Verbally attacking authority works well because most people enjoy seeing those they ordinarily defer to—the boss, police officer, faculty dean, politician—as the butt of a joke. *Saturday Night Live* can trace some of its popularity to this type of humor.

Finally, **laughing at ourselves** makes others laugh. Recalling the blunders you made the first time you appeared on television—how you kept watching the wrong camera and turning away from the microphone—might have humorous potential.

It can be helpful to memorize a few funny stories to use when the need arises. But remember, whether your use of humor is spontaneous or planned, it should always be in good taste and suited to the audience and the situation.

QUOTATIONS   Including some striking quotations can add interest to your responses. If you are well read, or at least well prepared, you can use the quotations to help make your point as well as to evoke interest. For example, if you were talking about hypocrisy in politics, you could use some of the following quotations to enliven your answers: "It makes no difference who you vote for—the two parties are really one party representing 4 percent of the people" (Gore Vidal). "Politics is the gentle art of getting votes from the poor and campaign funds from the rich, by promising to protect each from the other" (Oscar Ameringer). "Government is too big and important to be left to the politicans" (Chester Bowles). "Have you ever seen a candidate talking to a rich person on television?" (Art Buchwald). "We have the best politicians money can buy" (Will Rogers).

EVIDENCE   Make abundant use of the forms of evidence discussed in Chapter 3: illustrations, facts and figures, and testimony. A review of that material might be useful at this time.

VISUAL AIDS   We talked about their uses and advantages in Parts Four and Five and suggest you re-examine that material as it might apply to the television interview. Pointing to a chart or picture while you answer some questions could help explain your thesis while securing attention.

SUMMARY

Before the red light goes on, there is a moment of silence, you take a breath; the light goes on and the interview begins. If you've prepared yourself, then your primary concerns are now interacting, questioning and controlling.

We've talked about interaction in terms of listening and speaking. In listening it is important to pay attention, to be genuine, to remain involved, to take brief notes, to identify the main points, and to be motivated. In speaking it is important to state your main points, to be brief, to relate to your audiences, to be accurate, to avoid appearing smug or evasive, and to remain calm. As we have said, common sense and good manners should prevail in the interactions that take place in an interview.

Questions are also important in television interviews. Open, closed, hypothetical, probing and silent questions are common in television interviews. Knowing what kind of questions you are asking or answering is a key to a successful television interview.

Control in television interviews is as important as interaction and questioning. The participants in an interview control such visual elements as personal composure, dress, and gestures. Interviewers and interviewees also exert control of the message and interest values of their presentations.

PART
SIX

TELEVISION INTERVIEWS
REVIEW

Press, talk-show, and mediated are the most common forms of interviews in television. Each type involves a thousand factors, but interaction, questions, and control are central in any television interview.

In Chapter 12 we recommended preparing for an interview by doing your homework, knowing your purpose, understanding your options, understanding your rights, practicing, and getting ready mentally and physically.

In Chapter 13 we discussed interaction, questions, and control as ongoing processes of television interviews. In concluding our discussion, we reiterate the importance of common sense and good manners. They are the basis of our recommendations and clearly apparent in successful television interviews.

We would also reiterate that the interview entails every aspect of television presentation discussed in this book. We believe that to do a good interview of whatever type, it is necessary to understand the human factors involved. We also believe that doing a good interview requires commitment and organization on the part of both questioner and questionee.

RESOURCES

Notes

1. Jack Hilton and Mary Knoblauch, *On Television: A Survival Guide for Media Interviews* (New York: Amacon, 1980), p. viii.
2. Thomas Griffith, "Newswatch," *Time,* 6 June 1983, p. 55.

Recommended Readings

EINHORN, LOIS J.; PATRICIA HAYES BRADLEY; and JOHN E. BAIRD, JR. *Effective Employment Interviewing: Unlocking Human Potential.* Glenview, Ill.: Scott, Foresman, 1982.

MARTIN, DICK. *The Executive's Guide to Handling a Press Interview.* New York: Pilot Books, 1981.

MEDLEY, ANTHONY. *Sweaty Palms: The Neglected Art of Being Interviewed.* Belmont, Calif.: Lifetime Learning Publications, 1978.

SAMOVAR, LARRY A., and SUSAN A. HELLWEG. *Interviewing: A Communication Approach.* Dubuque, Iowa: Gorsuch Scarisbrick, 1982.

STEWART, CHARLES J., and WILLIAM B. CASH, JR. *Interviewing: Principles and Practices.* Dubuque, Iowa: Wm. C. Brown, 1978.

PART SIX

TELEVISION INTERVIEWS

KEY: 0 = Item does not apply
       1 = Extremely well done
       2 = Fairly well done
       3 = Moderately well done
       4 = Poorly done; needs improvement

CHAPTER 12. Preparing for the Television Interview

A. Understood types of interviews	0	1	2	3	4
1. Understood press interviews	0	1	2	3	4
2. Understood talk shows	0	1	2	3	4
3. Understood interactive systems	0	1	2	3	4
B. Understood the characteristics of television interviews (in general)	0	1	2	3	4
1. Understood purposes	0	1	2	3	4
2. Understood organization	0	1	2	3	4
3. Understood message exchange	0	1	2	3	4
4. Understood questions	0	1	2	3	4
5. Understood control	0	1	2	3	4
C. Use of the steps of preparation (in general)	0	1	2	3	4
1. Learned about the interview	0	1	2	3	4
2. Knew main purpose	0	1	2	3	4
3. Prepared some responses	0	1	2	3	4
4. Knew rights and exercised them	0	1	2	3	4
5. Practiced	0	1	2	3	4
6. Prepared physically and mentally	0	1	2	3	4

CHAPTER 13. Being Interviewed on Television (in general)

A. Listened carefully	0	1	2	3	4
1. Started listening from the start	0	1	2	3	4
2. Faked attention	0	1	2	3	4
3. Made effective use of speaking– thinking rate	0	1	2	3	4
4. Took notes	0	1	2	3	4
5. Identified speaker's main purpose	0	1	2	3	4
6. Was motivated	0	1	2	3	4
B. Stated main thesis early	0	1	2	3	4
C. Was brief	0	1	2	3	4
D. Related to viewers, not the interviewer	0	1	2	3	4
E. Was accurate	0	1	2	3	4
F. Didn't flaunt preparation and expertise	0	1	2	3	4
G. Wasn't evasive	0	1	2	3	4
H. Stayed calm	0	1	2	3	4
I. Use of language (in general)	0	1	2	3	4
1. Avoided jargon	0	1	2	3	4
2. Was accurate	0	1	2	3	4
3. Was vivid	0	1	2	3	4

	0	1	2	3	4
4. Avoided unnecessary verbal distractions	0	1	2	3	4
a. Avoided slang	0	1	2	3	4
b. Avoided clichés	0	1	2	3	4
J. Established and maintained credibility	0	1	2	3	4
1. By being experienced on the subject	0	1	2	3	4
2. By use of information	0	1	2	3	4
3. By being reasonable	0	1	2	3	4
4. By being organized	0	1	2	3	4
5. By demonstrating integrity	0	1	2	3	4
6. By being empathetic	0	1	2	3	4
7. By manifesting identification	0	1	2	3	4
K. Knew types of questions (in general)	0	1	2	3	4
1. Open-ended questions	0	1	2	3	4
2. Closed-ended questions	0	1	2	3	4
3. Hypothetical questions	0	1	2	3	4
4. Leading questions	0	1	2	3	4
5. Probes	0	1	2	3	4
6. Silence	0	1	2	3	4
L. Helped control the flow and direction of the interview (in general)	0	1	2	3	4
1. Was informed	0	1	2	3	4
2. Asked questions	0	1	2	3	4
3. Wasn't interrupted	0	1	2	3	4
4. Refuted incorrect statements	0	1	2	3	4
5. Corrected misinterpretations	0	1	2	3	4
6. Used transitions	0	1	2	3	4
7. Had the "last word"	0	1	2	3	4
M. Was interesting (in general)	0	1	2	3	4
1. Used examples	0	1	2	3	4
2. Was current and timely	0	1	2	3	4
3. Used humor	0	1	2	3	4
4. Used quotations	0	1	2	3	4

ISSUES IN THE USE OF TELEVISION

The only way to predict the future is to have the power to shape it.

Eric Hoffer

The personal use of television involves personal responsibility. We have touched on many issues in this book that are normally thought to be the concern of television executives, sponsors, and stars—but your personal and professional use of television necessitates that you personally deal with those issues. This overview returns to four issues that we said were particularly important in the individual use of television. Whether you want the responsibility or not, being on television means that you must deal with (1) objectives; (2) values; (3) control; and (4) substance.

OBJECTIVES

Having objectives is one of the more distinctly human characteristics of television communication. Electronic hardware does not have objectives beyond those imbued by its human masters. When we talk about objectives in television communication, we are talking primarily about *your* objectives. We noted earlier how objectives can confound and confuse human interchange; we suggested that it is important to understand programming, audience, and personal objectives.

Programming Objectives

You often have very little influence over programming objectives. Unless you own the system, you are a "guest," and usually must adhere to the objectives of the program. Make sure you understand them so that you can prepare and participate in an intelligent and effective manner. Being deadly serious on a lighthearted talk show would be out of sync with the program's objectives.

Audience Objectives

As we noted in Chapter 2, audiences as well as speakers have objectives—that is, people have a reason for watching television. A college class taking a chemistry course via a closed-circuit system has a different set of goals than does a group of friends watching reruns of *Saturday Night Live*. Think about your audience's objectives *before* you decide on your content and your style of delivery.

Personal Objectives

How well you identify your own objectives—be they to inform, persuade, or entertain—and how you make the necessary adjustments to accomplish them will determine whether you survive in the competitive world of television communication. Therefore, we urge you to think about your purpose for being on television and let it influence every phase of your preparation and presentation.

VALUES

As you attempt to accomplish your objectives, you must also develop a code of ethics. The increase in individual access to television does not automatically guarantee autonomy of expression. There has always been a tension between individuals and their societies. We think that every individual who steps in front of the camera feels that tension. The corporate executive videotaping a message for employees feels it as much as the person being interviewed on a talk show. Do you tell the whole truth? Do you allow all to be seen? Do you allow your "real" self to emerge? Do you bow to popular taste and beliefs? And how far?

These and other ethical questions must be confronted by anyone who appears on television. For whether you want to acknowledge the responsibility or not, what people see and hear on television can change the way they perceive reality. Richard Weaver clearly articulated this same point when he wrote, "We are all of us preachers in private or public capacities. We have no sooner uttered words than we have given impulse to other people to look at the world, or some small part of it, in our way."[1]

Because television is a mass medium, being on television can give you power and stature that may not have ever been yours in face-to-face encounters. You can see why we recommend pondering your ethical responsibilities when appearing on television. Have you and your message diminished the individual and human potentials of your viewers? Have you contributed to your viewers' emotional, spiritual, or mental well-being?

Bertrand Russell, in exploring individual and social values, felt that "without civic morality, communities perish; without personal morality their survival has no value."[2] The question, as Russell asked it, is, "How can we combine that degree of individual initiative which is necessary for progress with the degree of social cohesion that is necessary for survival?"[3] We do not have the complete answer. But we do know that the question is important to anyone using the medium of television.

CONTROL

We've discussed control throughout this book because we find it to be a central issue in television. Whether you're standing in front of the camera, behind the camera, or in front of your television set, controlling the medium is a challenge.

Thus far in our discussions of control we've focused on the personal and group levels of television communication—the speaker and the production crew. But the control of television, as a mass medium of human exchange, goes beyond a particular person or studio group. Economic and political controls shape television messages just as surely as speakers, equipment, and studio personnel do. Nor can control in television be adequately discussed without reference to audiences and their effects on the medium.

Our perspective in writing this book has been that you should focus on controlling your level, whatever that might be. If you're standing in front of the camera, then you control yourself as far as possible and take responsibility for your content, organization, delivery, and effects. If you're at home watching television, then you control the volume, tone, color, and channels at your command. It seems clear that everyone has some control of television, at some level.

Whether parents take responsibility for choosing the programs seen by children is a control issue. Whether a political state has the right to screen or block satellite transmissions is a control issue. Whether the producer, the director, the camera operator, or the speaker dictates how a program will be edited can be a control issue. How much control will you have? Will you share it? With whom? On what occasions will your control be increased or decreased? These questions must be asked and answered by anyone attempting to communicate effectively on television.

SUBSTANCE

In the '40s, television was black and white and deadly serious. Even the serials, though comedic in nature, tended to be taken seriously, as reflections of real human beings in real-life situations. In the '50s, television gained color, a mass audience, commercial clout, and banality. In the late '50s, Edward R. Murrow compared prime-time television to Nero fiddling while Rome burned.[4]

The banality of American television continued into the '60s. Newton Minow, at a meeting of the National Association of Broadcasters, called television a "vast wasteland"; the description has been widely quoted since.

As of the late '70s, television continued to offer pap rather than substance. In 1979 Edward J. Whetmore noted a continued "shift away from the importance of content to an increasing emphasis on form." He argued that "it is style, not substance, that will be the wave of the future."[5]

In our dealings with television, we have arrived at two observations about substance that lend perspective to the issue.

First, television does have *substance*. Anyone who uses television can see that television is not frivolous as some critics would have us believe. We have tried to stress throughout this text that reasonable and well documented television messages are part of this medium. Second, we believe that a change in access and in the availability of television time will lead to *more substantive* television fare in the future.

The Present

Our discussion in Chapter 3 demonstrated that television does have substance. Evidence and argument are very much apparent in television— not to the degree that some critics would like, but apparent nevertheless. It may be true that television is generally banal; the same might be said of most human communication. As we pointed out in Chapters 3 and 4, however, television can be, and often is, thought-provoking.

We believe that critics often miss the substance of television because they don't fully understand the medium. As we've continued to illustrate throughout this book, television is both aural and visual. A critic listening well might still miss the substance of a program by not integrating the sound with the sight.

In talking about logic and television we noted the study wherein arguments were composed of both visual and auditory parts. Not to see television as both visual and auditory is often to miss its logic. As we pointed out in our discussion on television scripting, television speakers must be aware of and integrate the audio and video columns of a script.

Programs like *Civilization, The Ascent of Man,* and *Cosmos* are clearly informative in nature and critically laudable for their substance. On the other hand, programs like *Hill St. Blues* and *One Day at a Time* are often dismissed as non-substantive because they are prime time, they appeal to a mass audience, and they seem predominantly entertaining and mundane. Such dismissal may be an error. Indeed, the distinctions made between the informing nature of *Cosmos* and the entertaining nature of *One Day at a Time* may be based on attitude rather than fact.

One Day at a Time is substantive in many ways. The program evidences and argues such contemporary issues as human sexuality, drug use, human relationships, and survival in urban units. A critic might conveniently lump *One Day at a Time* with most television programming and call such programming banal. But before such criticism can be taken seriously, the issues would have to be demonstrably false, the situations proven untenable. It's our belief that such demonstrations and proofs have been largely absent from television criticism and that most television criticism has been based on attitude rather than evidence and argument.

The Future

As we noted in the first chapter, television is available as a communication outlet to just about anyone. We suspect that one outcome of increased access to television will be increased substantiveness in television presentations, because of the increase in competition. This increased competition is a demonstrated economic fact. Cable television competes with traditional network television; satellite television competes with local cable systems; low-power television stations compete with high-power television stations.

We also base our optimistic outlook on the fact that as more people begin exploring television communication, a greater variety of expression will emerge.

We noted earlier that the introduction of audio cassettes brought contemporary sound technology to people who might not otherwise be able to afford it. They were integral in the New Wave music of the late '70s and early '80s. Portable and affordable television equipment could well lead to a "new wave" of television communication.

No one can be sure what that new wave will look like, but we speculate that it will, like the new wave of music, seem somewhat crude in its initial stages. Amateur efforts will abound; most of them will have embarrassingly poor production values. However, as with the new music, ideas, humor, and beliefs will emerge despite low-quality production.

As channel options increase, even amateur productions will have a chance at airtime. Of the millions of programs aired, some will evolve to the same level of quality of other human expressions cast in stone, print, and canvas.

We are obviously optimistic. We think that increased access to the medium of television will lead to both quality and quantity in television substance. Whether our optimism is justified depends on how well everyone adapts to the medium of television.

RESOURCES

Notes

1. Richard W. Weaver, "Language is Sermonic," in *Dimensions of Rhetorical Scholarship* (Norman, Okla.: Department of Speech, University of Oklahoma, 1968), p. 62.
2. Bertrand Russell, *Authority and the Individual* (New York: Simon and Schuster, 1949), p. 70.
3. *Ibid.*, p. 1.
4. Erik Barnouw, *Tube of Plenty* (New York: Oxford University Press, 1975), p. 237.
5. Edward Jay Whetmore, *Mediamerica* (Belmont, Calif.: Wadsworth, 1979), p. 312.

Recommended Readings

CASSATA, MARY B., and MOLEFI K. ASANTE. *Mass Communication: Principles and Practices.* New York: Macmillan, 1979.

CHAFFEE, STEVEN H., and MICHAEL J. PETRICK. *Using The Mass Media: Communication Problems in American Society.* New York: McGraw-Hill, 1975.

DAVIS, DENNIS K., and STANLEY J. BARAN. *Mass Communication and Everyday Life.* Belmont, Calif.: Wadsworth, 1981.

DEXTER, LEWIS ANTHONY, and DAVID MANNING WHITE, eds. *People, Society, and Mass Communications.* New York: The Free Press of Glencoe, 1964.

GUMPERT, GARY, and ROBERT CATHCART, eds. *Inter/Media: Interpersonal Communication in a Media World.* New York: Oxford University Press, 1982.

McLUHAN, MARSHALL. *Understanding Media: The Extensions of Man.* New York: McGraw-Hill, 1964.

MERRILL, JOHN C., and RALPH D. BARNEY, eds. *Ethics and the Press: Readings in Mass Media Morality.* New York: Hastings House, 1975.

NEWCOMB, HORACE, ed. *Television: The Critical View.* 3rd ed. New York: Oxford University Press, 1982.

NILSEN, THOMAS R. *Ethics of Speech Communication.* New York: Bobbs-Merrill, 1966.

PEMBER, DON R. *Mass Media Law.* Dubuque, Iowa: Wm. C. Brown, 1977.

PHELAN, JOHN, *Disenchantment: Meaning and Morality in the Media.* New York: Hastings House, 1980.

INDEX